# FIRED:

# FIRED:

HOW TO MANAGE YOUR CAREER IN THE
AGE OF JOB UNCERTAINTY

## Dr. Nancy Koury King

ISBN: 1978407130
ISBN-13: 9781978407138
Library of Congress Control Number: 2017916393
CreateSpace Independent Publishing Platform
North Charleston, South Carolina

# DEDICATION

*To my husband Dave and my children Kory and Eric, thank you for your unending belief in me, your encouragement and your inspiration.*

*To my parents Joe and Shirley Koury, thank you for always being there for me. I miss you.*

*To my siblings Linda Pantaleano, Joe Koury and Cindy Calvert, I am so grateful for your love and friendship.*

*To Paul Salipante, John Aram, Richard Boyatzis, Eileen Doherty-Sil, and Melvin Smith, I thought of you often writing this book. Thank you for teaching me.*

*To friends and colleagues who read drafts, gave advice, and provided moral support, I could not have done this without you.*

# CONTENTS

# INTRODUCTION AND OVERVIEW

"Work is about a search for daily meaning as well
as daily bread, for recognition as well as cash, for
astonishment rather than torpor; in short, for a sort of
life rather than a Monday through Friday sort of dying."
—STUDS TERKEL, *WORKING: PEOPLE TALK ABOUT WHAT THEY
DO ALL DAY AND HOW THEY FEEL ABOUT WHAT THEY DO*

Have you ever been laid off, let go, discharged, fired, or terminated from your job? Has your job ever been outsourced, replaced by technology, or eliminated by your employer? Has your company been acquired by another, causing downsizing and consolidation of positions? If so, you are not alone.

Getting fired or laid off is more common than you may think. According to the Bureau of Labor Statistics, about twenty-one million Americans (adjusted for seasonal workers) lost their jobs involuntarily in 2015.

Twenty-one million! And 2015 wasn't unusual. For the previous five years, the number of people let go or laid off from their jobs has ranged from 19.9 million to 21.7 million.

*Job insecurity may be the new normal.* Involuntary job loss can happen to anyone.

## What This Book Is About

To write this book, I spent more than five years interviewing and listening to dozens of people who were fired or laid off at least once; some of them had even experienced job loss two or three times. I listened carefully as people across the United States shared their stories of the actual firing experience, how they felt, how they coped and recovered, and in most cases, how they found new employment. I was curious to understand what if anything they learned and how they were different as a result of their experience. I was also interested in hearing what advice they might have for those who were currently employed or facing the same predicament. (For more information on the details of my research methods, see the appendix.)

I took inspiration from the book *Working* by Studs Terkel. With minimal commentary of his own, he let the oral histories of workers in America reveal their powerful, painful, and compelling experiences. "People are hungry for stories. It's part of our very being," he said.

*Working* illustrated the power of work in people's lives—the positive and the negative, the painful and the tedious. Working has incredible meaning and impact on our lives—both at home and at work.

In this book I tell the stories of people who were *not working*—those who were fired, laid off, or lost their jobs in some other way. As *Working* illuminated the impact of work in our lives, it is my hope that this book will shed light on the experience of involuntary job loss. What happens when this powerful force in our lives is taken away? How do people cope with and recover from this loss? I suspect most people are not prepared emotionally, occupationally, or financially for unexpected job loss. How do terminations affect families? What are the signs of impending job loss? What are some strategies for becoming reemployed? What are the lessons learned?

Most of all, I hope this book helps people who have experienced job loss and all the hardships associated with it and helps to prepare those who have not yet experienced job insecurity.

Instead of compiling a series of entire interviews, I organized the stories and excerpts into themes. The book is organized into three sections. Part 1 deals with the actual termination event and the aftermath. I share the verbatim stories of how people were told they were being let go, how they told their families, and how they felt emotionally. Part 2 contains their journeys toward recovery. Those I spoke with shared their personal, financial, and family hardships that resulted from the termination. They shared how they coped with the loss, the joblessness, and how they spent their time. They also shared their challenges both in job seeking and in starting a new position. Part 3 of the book is advice from the firing line. In hindsight, people recounted what they wish they had known and done while they were still employed. These insights and experiences could be invaluable to anyone currently in the workforce. They also have specific, detailed advice, both practical and philosophical, for those who are out of work and actively seeking it. I end the book with one simple question: What have you learned? What these individuals have gleaned on their difficult journeys may be helpful to others potentially or actually facing similar situations.

## What This Book Is Not

Although the focus of my research is on people who were fired, laid off, or whose job was eliminated, this book is not an attempt to vilify corporate America. It does not search for blame, nor is it an exposé.

With full intent, this book presents only one side of the story—that of the person being let go. As someone who has been on both the giving and receiving ends of the issue, I fully realize that there are many, many sides to any story. My goal in this book is not to diagnose or to prove or disprove the legitimacy of each termination or layoff. Nor is it to vindicate this study's participants or their employers. It is simply to tell the story of job loss from the perspective of the individual employee.

This is also not a book that proclaims the benefits of getting fired. It may be cliché to say that getting fired was the best thing that ever happened to a person. Two of the individuals I spoke with said just that, so for some it's true. There are books that tout this message and promote new beginnings and personal and professional growth. While some of the people I interviewed would say they were ultimately better off for having been fired, others would not. In her book *The Tumbleweed Society*, Allison Pugh describes job precariousness: "It's the engine for inequality because one-third of those that get laid off get work again at a comparable wage, doesn't get work, and makes less. People who get let go suffer wage decreases, and people who are hired back are hired back at less." This book is not one of those that take the motivational bent of "this is the best thing that ever happened to you."

Many books cover how to respond legally to being fired. They focus on such topics as employee rights (or lack thereof), discrimination, and employment at will. They may also explain how to best negotiate a departure. While some of the stories refer to these kinds of legalities, this book does not focus on the legal aspects of being fired and offers no legal advice.

This book does not dispense expert mental health information, so it will not help those seeking professional advice on how to recover emotionally from getting fired. I do share stories of the emotional toll getting fired has taken on our participants and their families. Many of them are still haunted by their termination. Those who were interviewed generously and intimately related the personal stories of their journeys to acceptance and recovery, and how they coped with the loss and were often able to become employed again. The stories and advice in this book are from those who have experienced being let go. Again, their opinions are not intended to be professional mental health advice or counseling.

Career counseling is a growing field. Many resources are available from career experts, outplacement counselors, and human resources professionals who give advice on how to find a job after being fired. While I have interviewed several professionals to provide background for this book, it is not a professional's how-to guide for getting back to work. Several of the people I spoke to took advantage of professional support and advice and shared their experiences. So while the book isn't a professional's recipe for landing on your feet, what you will find in this book is the invaluable advice from our participants on how to detect signals when your job is in jeopardy, and how to cope with the emotional roller coaster of being unemployed and trying to find a job. The interviewees freely offered their job-seeking tactics and their practical real-world tips. None of them claimed to be experts; they merely wanted to share their experiences to help others. Their advice is from the firing line, not the corporate office.

## Who Should Read This Book?

You may be wondering if this book is for you. It should be obvious that if you are out of work due to being laid off or fired, this book is definitely for you. You will hear stories of people who have experienced the shock, shame, anger, and depression of being let go. You will also hear their stories of coping and recovery. And importantly, you will hear what they have learned on this journey and their advice to others.

However, this book is just as much for those who are happily employed or have never experienced a job loss. Perhaps you are in a stable organization with a positive outlook for the future. You may not think this book is for you but rather a laid-off friend or family member. I would encourage you to think again. Several of the people in this research who shared stories of job loss were highly accomplished in their positions, had track records of success, and had positive performance evaluations. Many of them believed they were an important member of the organization, and some even had hopes of working there till retirement. They learned differently.

If you are an exempt employee, this book is for you. The fact is, employment at will is the law for exempt employees in most states. Employment at will means you can be fired for any or no reason at any time. In their book, *The Alliance: Managing Talent in the Networked Age*, authors Reid Hoffman, Ben Casnocha, and Chris Yeh call this the "fundamental disconnect of modern employment. Companies expect employee loyalty without committing to job security or professional development."

It may surprise you, but if you are a millennial, this book is for you. Millennials are at the beginning of their careers. "Ninety-one percent of Millennials (born between 1977–1997) expect to stay in a job for less than three years," according to the Future Workplace's "Multiple Generations @ Work" survey of 1,189 employees and 150 managers. That means they would have 15–20 jobs over the course of their working lives!" And recent articles and studies point out that millennials' attitudinal and behavioral expectations are getting them in trouble with their employers. According to J. T. O'Donnell in her *Inc.* magazine article "3 Reasons Millennials Are Getting Fired," "A backlash to Millennials' mindsets at work is causing some to get fired."

And this question is surprisingly important: Are you starting a new job? According to a study by Leadership IQ, which tracked twenty thousand new employees, 46 percent of new hires failed within the first eighteen months on the job. Many employers feel that their new hires don't work out because they can't handle the required responsibilities, but that is just a small part of why they don't succeed.

In his article "Hiring for Attitude: Research and Tools to Skyrocket Your Success Rate," Mark Murphy of Leadership IQ reported, "Even more surprising than the failure rate was that when new hires failed, 89% of the time it was for attitudinal reasons and only 11% of the time for a lack of skill. The attitudinal deficits that doomed these failed hires included a lack of coach-ability, low levels of emotional intelligence, motivation and temperament." Just like the high school lunch table, you don't always fit in. Regardless of the reasons, the odds are just about even for lasting beyond eighteen months in a new job.

This book will be helpful for people who have a new boss, as well as people taking on a new management position. It will call attention to the enormous influence that a new supervisor has on his or her employees and their job security. More than half of the people who were interviewed for this book lost their jobs after getting a new boss. This is an area where the company's leadership could have an impact on improving transitions.

Maybe you're a company executive or human resources professional. If so, this book is also for you. Firing someone is never easy. Layoffs are a fact in an ever-changing economy. Due to workplace safety, proprietary information, and legal concerns, there is practically a script for how to fire or lay off someone. This book goes beyond the script and may provide insight on better termination policies and employment practices. If anything, it underscores the need for clearer communication and more accurate performance reviews.

Recruiters and career and outplacement counselors will find this a rich resource to share with their clients. The book validates the importance of taking recruiter calls and examining career options from time to time. Career and outplacement counselors were recommended by many of the people I interviewed. These professionals can help their clients cope with the world of job insecurity by hearing about the experiences and advice of those interviewed for the book.

Those concerned about employee engagement, corporate culture, and the health of a company may also find this book useful. The bitterness and disenchantment of someone who has involuntarily lost a position can also be felt by that individual's coworkers and often has a negative impact on how much time and effort they will invest in a company. As Gallup Daily poll reveals, on March 5, 2017, only 33 percent of workers in America were engaged at work, meaning only a third of the nation's workers feel an emotional connection to their companies. For businesses and leaders attempting to create an engaged workplace culture, this book will provide many insights as well.

Professors of business, human resources, leadership, and management will find this book pertinent for their students. Research is sparse on being fired because it's a subject no one wants to touch. Yet it is a subject students want to understand. It is also difficult to locate people to be surveyed or interviewed who are recently fired and willing to be studied. According to Jone Pearce, author of *Organizational Behavior: Real Research for Real Managers,* "Most research on organizations focuses on the manager's perspective, and so research that takes the perspectives of the individuals who are affected is needed."

When they graduate and gain some experience, students of management and business are likely to be working in companies that at some time are faced with reductions in workforce, layoffs, and terminations. They may even be personally affected by workforce reductions and even dismissals. Students of management and business would benefit from understanding how terminations affect employees being let go as well as their remaining coworkers.

## Chapter Overview

Chapter 1, "The Firing Squad," details how people were laid off or let go. The experiences of the interviewees are organized by the different ways people were let go, from receiving a certified letter to being called into a meeting at four o'clock on a Friday afternoon, and the different reasons for being let go, from a downsizing or restructuring to being fired.

In Chapter 2, "Where There's Smoke, There's Fire," the study's participants recalled the period before they lost their jobs. They identified the signs that indicated they were about to be let go. Almost all of them said they were shocked or blindsided when they were terminated. However, in hindsight, almost everyone could identify some indicators that suggested the circumstances weren't normal.

Chapter 3 is titled "You're Not Fireproof." This chapter tells the stories of people who thought they would never be fired. Their experiences illustrate that despite an excellent work record, many years of service to the company, outstanding evaluations, promotions, and other forms of recognition, people can still lose their jobs.

In Chapter 4, "Fire Escape," I record the stories of those who recognized the signs before they were let go and took action to plan their exit.

Chapter 5, "Burn Notice," tells the stories of those who believe they were blackballed by their employer after they were terminated. They related the difficulty they had in finding another job within their company if their position had been eliminated or in another company—due to their employer signaling in some way that they were not a promising hire.

Chapter 6 is the last chapter in section one. "Fire-Exit Strategy" focuses on the importance of having an exit strategy and how an exit strategy can be formulated.

Section 2 examines the impact of job loss. Chapter 7, "Fire and Rain," focuses on the emotional impact. There are no neat, predictable phases of feelings. Rather, the people interviewed described a flood of emotions.

"Friendly Fire and Fire's Warmth" is the title of Chapter 8. As in other stressful times, people learn who their true friends are. Friendships were strained or ended for many people as a result of job loss. But that isn't the whole story. Those interviewed also experienced true acts of caring and friendship.

Section two concludes with Chapter 9, "Burn Unit Recovery." The interviewees shared how they coped with and recovered from their sudden job loss.

The third section offers advice based on participants' experiences. Chapter 10, "Fire Prevention Education," begins the section with advice to those who are *still employed.* In hindsight, the interviewees recounted what they wish they had known and done while they were still employed. These insights and experiences could be invaluable to anyone currently in or hoping to reenter the workforce.

Chapter 11, "Advice from the Firing Line," centers on the interviewees' specific and detailed advice for those who are unemployed and actively seeking a job.

In Chapter 12, "Burn Scars," you will learn how people who have experienced a job loss are different. How did they change as a result of being fired?

I concluded my interviews with one simple question: What have you learned? Chapter 13, "Lessons Learned from the Firing Line," lists some of the interviewees' responses to that question. The lessons learned as they navigated the realities and emotions of their difficult journeys may be helpful to those experiencing similar situations.

I asked myself the same question: What have I learned? Chapter 14, "Reflections," I add my own thoughts.

I owe a debt of gratitude to the individuals who shared their experiences with me. It was not easy reliving painful moments. Their experiences are the heart and soul of this book.

# PART 1

## THE FIRING EXPERIENCE

"The handwriting is on the wall."

"I was shaken, shocked. I knew after that I was a marked woman.
She was going to get me fired."

"I was told to clean my things out."

"How do I go from outstanding to terminated?"

# CHAPTER 1

## THE FIRING SQUAD: THE EXPERIENCE OF BEING FIRED

> I mean this sincerely now. The way [Trump] talks—
> think about growing up in your house at your kitchen
> table. If you ever talked about people like he does…
> if you ever sat there and talked about how cool it was
> that John down the street got fired ('You're fired,'
> a phrase [Trump has] made famous…), you ought
> to come from a household where some people were
> fired, where the plant closed down, where all of
> a sudden they're staring at the ceiling wondering
> "how in God's name am I going to make it."
> —VICE PRESIDENT JOE BIDEN,
> SEPTEMBER 1, 2016, WARREN, OHIO

In his reality-television shows *The Apprentice* and *The Celebrity Apprentice*, now-President Donald Trump made the catchphrase "You're fired" infamous. The television show became a window to what previously was a private discussion. Mr. Trump would gather contestants together and ask them to identify who they thought should be fired. After hearing from the contestants and consulting with his judges, he would point to someone at the end of each show and declare, "You're fired." The contestant would be escorted out and sent home packing. Of course, this was a reality TV show and not a normal employment setting. But the audience was able to view many things that happen in real firings: subjective

3

performance appraisals, perp walks out the door, and the emotional reactions of those fired. America was fascinated. The TV show opened its
first year in 2004 and remains in production as of 2017. Clearly, America
is interested in people being fired.

This book begins with the act itself—the actual firing. "How were
you fired?" is the first question I asked the people who shared their stories with me. If you've never been fired or laid off, or haven't had to fire
anyone, you may not know what happens in an actual job termination.
Even if you have, there is no single or uniform way people are terminated. Despite the professional advice of how to fire someone appropri-
ately (see the end of this chapter), the stories of the people interviewed
indicate quite a bit of variation.

I asked each person to describe how he or she was let go. Their
stories were amazingly clear and full of details covering the who, what,
when, where, and how.

Since most firings are done in private, it is difficult to study them.
But there have been many public and unceremonious firings. In May
2017, then FBI Director Comey was speaking to his bureau in California.
There was a TV screen on in the room. The audience listening to Comey
could see the TV screen's flashing announcement that Comey had been
fired. They let him know, and he thought it was a prank until he himself
saw the television screen. Comey was fired publicly, and adding insult to
injury, in front of his employees.

In 2013, Tim Armstrong, the CEO of AOL, fired Abel Lenz, a creative
director for AOL's Patch local-news business, in front of other coworkers
while one thousand employees listened in on a conference call to discuss
changes at the unit, including layoffs and site closings. Armstrong can
be heard saying on a recording of the meeting, "Abel, put that camera
down right now! Abel, you're fired. Out!" He then paused before continuing the meeting.

And President Ronald Reagan declared "You're fired" to the nation's
workforce of air traffic controllers, who were on strike. Reagan treated it
as a matter of national safety and ordered the striking air traffic controllers back to work. Those who did not return, more than eleven thousand
workers, were fired.

Job-loss notifications rarely take place on such a public platform as national television or business conference calls. However, the experiences of the people in this study ranged from the perfunctory to the outrageous.

In this chapter, I'll introduce you to some of the people interviewed. Here, they recount one small piece of their stories—how they learned they were no longer employed. More details of their experiences and those of others as well as the aftermath unfold throughout this book.

## Downsizing, Restructuring, Position Eliminated

> "I was told they were eliminating my position. Six weeks
> later I saw an ad for the same job I was just fired from."
>                                                    —KARL

Whether due to a merger, consolidation, technology, or outsourcing, many of those interviewed indicated that they weren't fired per se, rather their position was eliminated or the company had a restructuring or a reduction in workforce. Downsizing and restructurings do happen, and here are some examples. However, it is also true that there are actually firings disguised as reductions in workforce.

Lee, in his midforties, worked in the technology field. He was laid off from his position after only a year. This was his second time being let go. He had previously owned a small business, but when the economy turned, he went to work at a small branch of a large technology firm. He shared, "Human resources asked me to come into their office. They said I was being let go because business was bad and they couldn't support my position. They were downsizing. That is probably true. None of the bids were getting accepted. The boss was adding a 15 percent price increase to all of them on top of my bids. My bids were right-on. Then they marked them up. But they didn't try to block my unemployment benefits. That was good." However, you will hear later that Lee went to human resources with a complaint about a supervisor. He believes his

5

termination, while labeled a position reduction, was really retaliation and he was set up to be fired.

Another person who lost a job due to downsizing is Brenda. She had worked for the same organization for several years. "The reason I was given was that I was part of a downsizing. We were merging, and we cut fifty positions. That is what I was told. Clearly, it wasn't that at all. Everyone who was being downsized knew it. They had time to adjust. They got outsourcing help. They had notice. We knew there were fifty. I wasn't on the list, and I knew I wasn't.

"My boss came in at three o'clock on a Friday with a great big grin on her face and said, 'You're done. You have been downsized. Good luck.' I had two hours to get out. I knew I wasn't downsized—I had seen the list. She just used it as an excuse to get rid of me. After I got fired, five department heads of the company called me and said, 'What happened?'"

There are legitimate cases of companies downsizing out of necessity: a drop in business, a lack of profitability, or a change in company focus. Some of our interviewees were a part of these legitimate though difficult business transactions. For example, Derek worked for a large national retail chain. When his wife found work in another state, Derek was able to stay in the company and transfer to his new location. Four months after his transfer, the organization told its employees that it had planned layoffs. They planned to lay off half their department managers. However, the organization told its employees they had a job for a year—maybe not in their same position, but somewhere in the company.

But like Lee and Brenda, several interviewees shared that downsizing is often an excuse for letting someone go.

Another example comes from Andy, who watched others in his company lose their jobs. "They called it restructuring due to financial issues that had occurred earlier in the year because of the loss of a big client. So it was in the works. The senior vice president was moved out of the business unit, then three directors on the same day, and sixty more people two to three weeks later."

In his early forties, Andy had been in the communications business at this company for sixteen years. "My boss, with a person from HR, booked time with me the day before I was let go. It seemed suspicious. Ninety minutes before, the meeting got updated to a *mandatory attendance*. That had never happened before. 'Sorry, your role has been restructured' and 'here's HR to talk you through the next steps.'" Like others interviewed, he later learned they hired someone to take over his position.

Andy describes the humiliating end to his sixteen years at this company. "I wasn't allowed to go back to my desk. They walked me to my car, took my pass away, and told me to schedule time with Employee Assistance to come back to clear out my office." Being escorted out the door without being able to return to your workstation, collect your things, or say goodbye is known as the *perp walk*. A common practice in human resources is to not allow the individual to return to his or her office. Concerns include worrying that the person being let go might steal company property, cause an emotional scene, or even become violent.

Karl worked as a project manager at a large university. "I was told they were eliminating my position. Six weeks later I saw an ad for the same job I was just fired from."

Despite being told the company was in financial stress and had to reduce its workforce, both Andy and Karl discovered the painful truth that their companies were hiring new people for their positions after they left.

Earlier Lee described his second experience of being let go. His first experience came four years before when he was in his early thirties. He had worked at a communications company for six years. "I had just gotten married. My wife and I came back from our honeymoon, and there was a voice message from a coworker on our home phone waiting for me. He said things didn't look good for our jobs. He told me to be sure to check out Friday's paper when we returned. This was before smartphones. We managed to find a paper and the headline was that the company was going to have massive layoffs. I went in to work that Monday. They called us into a meeting room by groups. The person told us we were losing our jobs. We were each given a box and told to clean out our desks. The thing is, I had just been promoted to a specialized team. Had I stayed in my old job as a technician, I probably would have still had a job."

Like Lee, Nick also learned for the second time that he and his team were being let go. "My boss's contract wasn't renewed. He gathered us to assure us *he* would be OK. We knew he would be fine, but what about us? An interim leader came in to work with us. I asked him if he was planning to make any changes. He said he didn't know and not to worry about it. I had just been given an award for my record-breaking work. I called his counterpart in another organization. He told me that my interim leader had called him to let him know I was being let go. My counterpart told him he couldn't make the decision unilaterally since I was technically on the payroll of both companies. So that's how I found out. I started looking for another job. I went back to my supervisor and confronted him. I asked him about my team. I said, 'What if Joe is about to buy a new house?' thinking the team would want to have the information before they made any major life decisions. He said nothing. I found a new job. My first week there I received a letter addressed to me at my office from my former employer saying I was fired."

Sometimes people find out about a potential job loss through the media. Others, as you will read later, find out through coworkers. In many cases the employee is surrounded by people who know they are about to lose their jobs. In chapter 3 you will hear some of the signs of impending job loss.

## New Sheriff in Town

One of the most striking commonalities of the participants in this study was that the majority of them were let go shortly after there was a change in leadership or they got a new boss. While this is somewhat expected for C-suite positions, being let go after getting a new boss happened across the board, to employees at all job levels.

For example, Nick's first experience with job loss was due to an unexpected change in leadership. He had worked at a large organization for fifteen years. His boss was let go after being promised a promotion. "I was asked to meet with my boss's replacement, who was already in line as she was part of the transition. I walked into the room with my agenda, and she started by saying, 'I enjoy working with you, but your job is going to be eliminated.' She advised, 'I would utilize your remaining time to find your next great opportunity.' No offer of assistance. No mention of another opportunity at the company. 'I think the best thing for you to do is to pack up at the end of the month and don't come back. But use the time to work from home and find a job.'

"My next visit with her was after Thanksgiving, and she invited me into the office. She said, 'We don't need your position anymore.' I said I hoped I could bring value to the company with it, but understood each leader makes their own choices. I assumed I would be offered a position in my old department. I brought up my going back to my former position. She said no.

"I met with her boss, the person who got the promotion my boss was promised. I said I understood that my position wasn't going to be continued, and I wanted to talk to him about going back to my old department. I said I knew there were other positions, and I thought I had something to contribute. She just avoided eye contact and said goodbye."

Unfortunately, Joe has had several experiences of being let go from health-care organizations. "I applied to be the president of the organization; this was the time when I could make the leap. I was well entrenched. If I didn't do it, I would always wonder. I went for it. The CFO, who I had recruited to the organization, and I were the finalists. We both went through the process. I didn't get the position and the CFO did. She was a local person. My wife and I had a vacation planned. The new president had a few meetings planned for the week we were to be away, but we had already rescheduled once because of work. We went to China and had the greatest time. Then when we got back, at the end of the week, I got called to the president's office. She was late, so I waited; I was jittery. The president and board chairman came in. I said to myself this is not going to be good. She told me I wasn't what she had expected. I could take a demotion or take severance and leave."

Like Nick and Joe, you'll hear stories of employees who were caught in the wake when a new leader arrived in their organization. Despite their positive track record and tenure with the organization, they were not provided the opportunity to assimilate into the new leader's team.

## Not a Good Fit

When trying not to give a reason for termination or get into an argument about performance, companies often use the phrase "You're not a good fit." A similar euphemism is, "We're taking a new direction." Both of these phrases are obtuse and difficult to refute. Melissa worked for five years in a sales management position. "I got an e-mail from my boss with no subject line telling me when and where to come to a meeting. I went to the meeting room. My boss and HR were there waiting. My boss said they needed a 'change in direction.' I thought to myself, 'You need a change from year over year growth?' They said they had a severance agreement for me. To get my earned vacation they wanted me to give them a noncompete contract, which would have prohibited me from working in my field for a year. I couldn't do that."

Brenda shared a second time she was let go: "I had an appointment with my supervisor to do my evaluation. At 8:30 a.m. she came into my office and said, 'I'm firing you.' 'On what basis?' I asked. 'It's no longer a good fit.' So I was perp-walked out of that office. I was told I could come in Saturday with human resources and clean out my office."

An employer will use phrases like these to avoid being challenged and having to give explanation. Job-related performance issues can be refuted, or challenged, or explained. An employee has little recourse when told they are no longer a fit. It's like being told you can't sit at the popular kids' table in the middle school cafeteria. There are no criteria; the harsh reality is they just don't want you.

## Don't Tell Anyone

> "Well, I wanted to be working, so I agreed to
> keep my impending job loss a secret."
> —CAROL

In a few cases, people I interviewed were instructed not to tell others they were losing their job. In other words, the company wanted to keep the employee's future departure a secret. Carol's story is an example. "The stock market and the economy were down, and it was affecting our business. Our boss pulled his team together to tell us there would be some belt tightening. We understood and were willing to reduce our costs."

Carol paused and continued, "Sometimes it's better to keep your mouth shut, and she couldn't do that. We were all nervous and anxious.

There were lots of questions about how we were going to cut costs. In an effort to reassure us, she said, 'No one is going to lose their job.'

"Big sigh of relief. OK, I thought, that's good. We can get through this. Two weeks later she and my boss asked to meet with me. They told me my job would be eliminated. But she had said no one would lose their job! Now I was given two months' notice—and I could either leave and take a pay out or stay on until the end of those two months. But the catch was I was not allowed to tell anyone. Well, I wanted to be working, so I agreed to keep my impending job loss a secret.

"And I wanted to get my employees situated. I also knew it would be easier to find a job if I had one. But they told me I couldn't tell anyone I was being let go! So I didn't. I didn't even tell my family. How hard is that—to be told your job is eliminated but not be able to tell anyone? I was treated so poorly."

Like Carol, Bruce was also asked not to tell people about his planned termination. He explained how he was let go after ten years of leading a community foundation. "Well, there was a board meeting scheduled right before the scholarship awards banquet. I was prepared to give a speech. Immediately the board went into session, and I was excused. An hour and a half later, I was brought back in. Most of the board members were on their way out, and we hadn't met yet. One of them said to me, 'There are a lot of people in that room who love you.' 'That was odd,' I thought.

"But then when I sat down, I saw that only the chair and a lawyer were in the room. I was told that I was no longer employed. They said I was being let go, but wanted me to stay until the end of the scholarship awards banquet. I said, 'I can't pretend—I don't think so!' and I left."

Unlike Carol, Bruce was unwilling to keep up the façade that everything was going well. He could not imagine how they expected him to act like nothing happened while knowing his job was over.

"One day you're a trusted leader and the next you feel like a criminal. You are a trusted employee, and the next day you are not trusted for anything. I get it: it is the standard way of firing people. Do you have to behave that way to someone who is a colleague?"

In her book *Organizational Behavior: Real Research for Real Managers*, Dr. Jone Pearce writes that the act of firing can be very painful for the firing manager. She states, "While this distress is natural, it often leads managers to try to get rid of these painful feelings as quickly as possible, hustling the shamed and stigmatized departing employees out the door immediately."

You will read throughout this book about false assurances, broken promises, and even bald-faced lies. And repeatedly, people wondered how they could be valued and recognized one day and fired the next day. Insensitive and degrading departures you will see not only cause pain for the person being let go, but for their remaining coworkers as well.

## You're Not Happy Here

> "And the division leader began to tell me he
> didn't think I was happy there anymore."
> —ELIZABETH

Another way to terminate someone is to make it look like it is in his or her idea or in his or her best interests. Janice had been with her company for fifteen years. "I got an e-mail saying to meet my boss and HR at four o'clock. No subject line. I was very suspicious. I thought they were going to fire me. I got to the meeting, and they told me people have noticed that I have checked out and look disinterested. I was so mad. I had been working night and day. I did not take a vacation last year and wanted to use my vacation for this year. I thought if they fired me, I would lose all my vacation pay. That's what happened to a good friend who also worked there. We were short staffed. I said, 'I can't do it alone.' My boss said, 'Is there anything we can do?' Before I could answer, the human resources manager said, "Shall we look at how can we part ways?' She was happy. This is what she wanted. He wanted me to stay, but she wanted me to leave. She had the power. So I had to leave."

Elizabeth worked in finance for a big box chain. "I was at the company thirteen years. So I had no clue I was losing my job. *No clue!* I got an e-mail from my division head saying that he wanted to see me at

4:00 p.m. I had an uneasy feeling about this. It was just the wording in the e-mail: 'Hey, can we meet and talk about financials?' I thought it was strange he wanted to talk to me about finance operations since he was the division leader.

"At lunchtime I called my husband. 'Something is not right; they are going to let me go.' He said, 'That's not happening; you are great.' I told him about the e-mail. He said it was going to be OK. When I walked into the division head's office, the human resources person was sitting there. I was thinking to myself, 'This is not good.' And the division leader began to tell me he 'didn't think I was happy there anymore.' He didn't think I would be a good fit for the new company that we would be outsourcing some work to. He felt it was best that we separate. I was taken aback.

"HR proceeded to go over the paperwork. He said I would need to pack up things and leave now. He said I had the option of her walking me out or someone else. I said I would prefer someone else. Scott was there—on standby—waiting in HR's office. She told him to escort me out.

"The HR person said, 'Elizabeth, let it out if you need to." I said, 'It's OK.' Scott asked, "What the hell is going on?" I said, 'They just let me go.' He said, 'You're shitting me.' I picked up my stuff at the office. I reached to log off my computer, and he said I couldn't touch the computer. I grabbed my coat and handbag and walked out the back door."

## They're Posting Your Job

> "Did you put an ad online for my job?"
> —Jeannie

On a few occasions, participants found out they were losing their jobs because they found a job posting that sounded a lot like their own position. This can happen when managers are trying to line up a replacement before letting someone go. It also happens when layoffs are pending, making employees compete for the remaining positions.

Jeannie had a midlevel management position in a human services organization. "I was looking at jobs on Indeed one Sunday and found a job that seemed a lot like mine. It was a blind ad, so I couldn't tell what the company was. I showed the posting to my boss the next day and asked, 'Did you put an ad online for my job?' At least she was honest, finally, and said yes, she did. She told me they didn't want to fire me until they had someone in place. I was furious."

In her early forties, Erica worked in logistics at a warehouse. Four of her coworkers received letters saying they would be laid off in three months. The letters went on to say that if they stayed for the full three months, they would get some extra vacation pay. Erica had a different job and did not receive a letter. She assumed she was not part of the layoffs. A month later she and her coworkers were called into their manager's office. They were told that the four employees who were going to be laid off were now able to compete with Erica for *her* job.

Shocked and angry, Erica asked to meet with her manager one-on-one. She said she was upset to learn about this in a meeting with her coworkers. Her manager was not responsive. She then asked if she would be given the same letter saying that if she remained on the job for three months she would get the additional pay. Her manager said, "No, that deal is not available for you." Then she asked her manager what she would do if one of the other employees was picked for her job. The manager said, "You will resign." Erica was not selected and was forced to resign.

Married with three school-age children, Renee had worked in a manufacturing company for over twenty years. During that time, she had received many promotions and even an award. She also had special training in process improvement and was liked by the team she supported, and her boss and her boss's boss were supportive of her work. Then things changed.

"My boss left the company, and I considered returning to my former position. It was open, and I could have gone back to it. I was worried about how things would go with a new boss. My boss's boss called to ask me not to go back to my old job, but to stay in my current role. She gave me the impression that she was looking out for me, that she wanted me in this department.

"A new boss started. She was recruited from the outside to come to the company and made claims that she could significantly increase its profitability. One day I was home after work and a friend called. She asked me if I was leaving my job. I said, 'No, why?' The friend told me there was a job posted online recruiting for what looked like my position. She said, 'They posted your position.' I said, 'Read it to me.' It was my job.

"The posting occurred before the boss had talked to me. Two other positions were posted too, and both described the jobs of current employees. Then my boss scheduled a conference call with me and two of my colleagues. She let us know she was going to have three positions in her department and the three of us 'may or may not get them.' She sent us a new organizational chart. Beside each of our names was an asterisk with the note *may or may not be in this position.* I asked, 'Will we keep our jobs?' My boss said we could apply for our positions but weren't guaranteed to get them."

As mentioned above, managers sometimes make an employee compete for his or her own job. This may relate to a workforce reduction or be a way for a new manager to pick his or her own team. It also provides the vehicle to demonstrate that everyone had an "equal chance" of being hired, even though sometimes managers have already made up their minds about who they're going to hire. In other cases, a manager places a blind ad or works with a recruiter to identify a candidate for a position before terminating the incumbent. This allows the organization to minimize the disruption in work. You will hear more from people who learned about their impending job loss through seeing their position posted or advertised.

## Leaves of Absence

> "They let me go on Friday knowing
> I had surgery on Tuesday."
> —DIANE

It surprised me to learn about participants in this study being let go when they were beginning, ending, or in the middle of a medical leave.

In her early fifties, Connie worked at the same law firm for twenty-eight years. She shared how she was notified that she would lose her job: "I was on medical leave after knee replacement surgery. While I was at outpatient physical therapy, I got a call. They had a private investigator call me. She said she tried to have a letter delivered to my house and asked when I would be home, so I told her. The delivery person said, 'You don't see this coming.' The letter said they had 'released me from probation.' I had taken on a new job with the same company right before my surgery. So technically I was on ninety-day probation. That meant they could release me for any reason.

"Even though I had been with the organization for twenty-eight years, and all my evaluations had 'exceeds expectations,' I was considered new and on probation. My first week, I attended a seminar. Then I was in the office two weeks before I went on leave for my knee replacement surgery. Two weeks later I got the notice: I am relieved from probation. That means I'm fired." A probationary period is common as some companies who want to underscore employment at will. This practice translates into treating an internal transfer or promotion the same as an external person coming into a job. Often an evaluation comes at the end of the probationary period.

Another participant, Diane, described the situation that led up to her termination "My boss came to me and talked about extending our business into another county and wanting my number-two person to do it. Something got misinterpreted in the communication. He said I behaved unprofessionally. He suspended me without pay for two weeks. Our policy states that the most one can be suspended is three days. He accused me of telling my employee about the position while the information was confidential. I didn't. I told her after the job was posted. *He wouldn't let me explain.*

"I went into a tailspin. I went to counseling every day to try to figure out what I was doing wrong, what I needed to do differently. Every day. I wrote a letter asking if I could use personal leave so I could get paid. I needed the money for my family. He said no. I had accrued six weeks of vacation. So I requested it, and he denied it. After two weeks I went back; I kind of buried my feelings.

"He kept saying I should run the program as I see fit. He said I was 'a rat on the wheel.' I wrote him a plan showing him I understood what he wanted. I admitted to myself that a drastic measure was needed. My aunt had just died. I was low. I wrote a very accommodating letter to him. I took all the blame and fault myself. I underwent stress management and grief counseling. I thought it was me. I thought it was all my fault.

"Then he showed up with HR at my office at the end of the day on a Friday. He said he wanted to restructure. He and HR laid it out for me. Basically my position was being eliminated. 'It's not a reflection on you,' they said. But later I learned that he didn't eliminate the job; he hired his friend.

"They knew about my history of breast cancer and that I was going into surgery for reconstruction. How was I going to pay for it? They knew it. It was horrible. They continued my insurance. The HR person I worked with didn't come; her number-two came. They let me go on Friday knowing I had surgery on Tuesday."

"I was on maternity leave," Gail recounted. "Prior to that there was a lot of triangulation going on between two other senior leaders and myself. I was the change agent. It became them against me. I knew something was up because neither one of them was in touch with me at all while I was on maternity leave.

"I found out something they were going to do just before I returned. It was something that should have involved me. I was excluded; it was intentional and pretty big. I called the boss to check in to let him know I was coming back the next day and was curious about the issue. 'Can you give me a heads-up?' He lost it. He screamed at me. I don't remember the words. I held the phone out the car window he was screaming so loudly. I said, 'OK, I'll see you tomorrow.'

"I went home and said to my husband, 'He's going to fire me.' My husband said, 'He can't do that; you are on maternity leave.' I said, 'Maybe not immediately, but he will fire me.'

"My first day back he asked to see me. I went to his office. He spoke well-rehearsed words. No one from human resources was present. He had a script. He was clearly agitated and working very hard to keep his composure. And I stayed calm. He said, 'We can do this one of two ways. You can leave right away, or you can stay here sixty to ninety days and look for a job while you are here.' I said, 'Are you firing me?' He said. 'You need to move on.' He said that three or four times. 'Well,' I said, 'I would like the night to think about it.' When I probed, he would not give me any reason. He just said, 'It's time to move on.' I was confused and intrigued about the timing and the level of anger on his part. And it felt very personal, and it was very personal."

A number of abrasive, insensitive terminations are described in this book. Letting someone go as he or she starts, takes, or returns from medical leave seems like a particularly egregious act. However, it is easier to plan a termination if the person is not in the office. It takes preparation, planning, and coordination to terminate someone. With the person out of the office, he or she will not be able to detect the changes in patterns of interaction or other signs that job loss is imminent. And it is easier for managers to not have to face the person terminated, so doing so right before he or she is going on vacation or on medical leave assures that the individual will not be around to engage with other employees or return to the office.

## You Told Your Boss You Plan to Quit

> "Telling your boss you plan to quit is like telling your girlfriend that you want to see other people. It doesn't go over well and often ends in a breakup."
> —ROB, FRIEND OF THE AUTHOR

Thinking they were being ethical and transparent, some of the interviewees approached their bosses to say they realized it wasn't working out and that they were going to look for a new position. They expected their supervisors to welcome the admission or at least be relieved. They were surprised to find their bosses' reactions so harsh.

Married with three children, Sam had worked for several years for an electronics company. A new boss had joined the firm, and Sam quickly ascertained that the two of them weren't going to work well together.

Sam decided to take the high road. "I went to my boss. I told him that I could see we weren't going to work well together. I said, 'We're both adults, so I am letting you know I will start looking for a new position.'" Sam thought that opting out was his best option. Unfortunately, his boss did not wait until Sam had found a job. "The week of Christmas I was fired. I had to call my wife, who had already left with the kids on vacation, and tell her I lost my job."

Randy had a similar story. He told his employer that he was going to move on. "Once I said, 'Let's make the change,' it moved quickly. I offered to continue working while looking for another job. My boss said no. I was out." Randy offered to work while they looked for his replacement, the company declined the offer, and Randy was out before he was ready to leave.

## Your Contract Wasn't Renewed

Employment contracts were in place for a few of the participants in the study. After a career in civil service, Mackenzie went to graduate school to become a teacher. She eventually found work in a small private school. To make extra money, she would babysit for several of the parents. She became close to one family. Mackenzie admits that she made a comment about another child in class to the child she was babysitting. The child told her parents and the other child. Soon the parents complained to the principal, who did not renew her contract for the next year. "I also had to write a public letter of apology. It was wrong, but I got so close to these people, and I let my guard down."

As head of his organization, Jonathan was faced with a difficult challenge. His organization was losing money and would have to do something drastic to get it back into financial shape. He consulted with his board of directors. They advised selling one of the properties in order to improve their cash position. Jonathan carried out the directive and sold the property. At the end of the year, much to his surprise, his contract was not renewed. He learned that one of his board members did not want the property sold, which happened to be in the city where that board member lived. Apparently Jonathan unknowingly killed a sacred cow, and was let go for doing so.

Mackenzie and Jonathan each knew the reasons their contracts were not renewed. For most of the people I interviewed, this was not the case.

## You're Fired

Mark was recruited to an organization after working many years for a nearby competitor. "I was served a letter that said resign or be fired. My boss handed it to me in a meeting. It was open, and he handed it to me. It spelled out my situation—that if I didn't resign, I wouldn't keep my benefits: my bonus, my vacation pay, and my paycheck covering the rest of month. They told me I could work out the resignation notice if I wanted. They also said I couldn't talk about it. If I didn't resign, they would fire me, and I would get none of those things.

"Once it was all revealed, there was a sense of flush. It wasn't emotional, it was deadening. It was real. It hit me. I went sullen. I didn't cry. I didn't get upset. Then my mind was on how to get myself out of there. I didn't want to be escorted to the door. I didn't want to have my stuff boxed. I said I would work the rest of the week. I used the rest of the week to pack up my stuff."

A recent graduate from a prestigious college, Sondra shared her experience of being fired from her first real job: "It happened to me on the day I was supposed to get my own desk. Up until then I worked at a folding table. I was all excited to get my own desk! As I was heading to where my desk was supposed to be, completely out of the blue I was pulled into HR. My boss was there. She said, 'We just don't think you're getting it.' As I held back my tears, they said, 'Grab your coat and leave.' I had already put all my personal stuff in bags, because I was getting my new desk. They said they would mail my things."

Don described how a promising beginning turned into a painful experience of being let go: "During the interview process, my future manager had a closed-door meeting with me where he confided that he was on the fast track and slated to move up the ladder with the department manager and that I was to be groomed as his replacement. I accomplished several important tasks and even solved a difficult problem my manager was working on, allowing him to take credit and run with the ball.

"After the first year the pressure exponentially increased. My manager absolutely had to climb the ladder. I took on more responsibility and was soon working fourteen-hour days, only taking off Christmas day itself. Then the department manager began zeroing in on me. He set up a series of weekly meetings and began mentoring me. I felt incredibly intimidated, as if I were under the microscope (I was). How could I, the new guy from outside the industry, come in and tell the others how to do what they had been doing in some cases for over twenty years?

"I kept up my performance as a project manager, but I certainly felt challenged to take over the group with confidence. One evening, well after most had gone, I was informed I was being put on a PIP (personal improvement plan). I had no idea what a PIP actually was and had to look it up. I suddenly got the seriousness of my predicament and vowed to fight like hell to keep this job at any cost. I went into hyperdrive and worked like a bandit.

"My manager and department manager notified me that they were preparing a very intense exam to prove my skills. I was given the exam a week later with a three-week deadline. This was in addition to my regular workload. My family realized the stress I was under and gave me the freedom to work as necessary to meet the demands. I worked nights, weekends, and early mornings—every moment balancing the two: the exam and my workload. This happened three times.

"One day I was preparing a presentation for the next day, and people kept coming into my office just to chat. I could hardly get anything done and kept ushering them out. After lunch about 2:00 p.m.—I call this 'the moment'—both my manager and department manager showed up at my door with a fistful of papers. Time actually seemed to slow. My department manager was smiling ear to ear—the smile of a long-sought victory—while my direct manager was sullen. I was told that if I didn't sign these papers in acknowledgment, I would not receive my final pay and some other benefits and that it would all work out the same anyhow, so for the betterment of my family I should sign. My face was flush with embarrassment. I, a hard-working, honest guy, was being fired. Our department manager apologized that this took so long and happily disappeared. No mention or sign of the HR department. I think they may have played this card without HR being completely on board, possibly notifying them later.

"My manager stepped across the hall and returned with boxes prepared. He made me collect all my personal things, watching every move. I asked if I could collect my gym things, so a security guard showed up and walked us to the gym. I felt everyone looking at me, and my embarrassment grew. I could hear pounding in my ears."

## You're Fired, and You Have to Train Your Replacement

As much as it hurts to be fired, being forced to train your replacement rubs salt into the wound. I spoke to a young serviceman whose mother was being let go. Her company was outsourcing her job to another country. Before she left, she had to train her replacement. In addition, recall that when Karen started her position, the person she was replacing had been asked to stay to train her, which was uncomfortable for both parties.

The television show *60 Minutes*, originally airing March 19, 2017, did an investigation on Americans who lost their jobs to less expensive foreign workers and then were required to train them. The companies deploying this practice were using a legal loophole in the H-1B visa program to hire highly skilled foreign workers to displace and replace more costly America workers. Adding insult to injury, the displaced workers had to train their replacements in order to get severance pay. The companies used the euphemism "knowledge transfer" rather than the blunt term *training*.

## No Due Process: Falsely Accused

"I can't sign because it isn't true."
—LORI

In several instances, interviewees were falsely accused of wrongdoing and were not given the opportunity to set the record straight. No due process or opportunity to appeal was afforded.

A recent college graduate, Alexa, twenty-two, was let go only three months after starting her first post-college position. During her termination meeting, she was accused of leaving work early, which she adamantly denied. She did recall that her teammates would tell her they were taking off early on occasion and encouraged her to do the same. "We're all leaving early, why don't you," her teammates would suggest. She now knows she was set up. Likewise, Lee reports being confronted by HR for "falsifying his time card." The HR manager said they had video proof. Lee explained that his supervisor instructed the team to leave early when he wanted to leave early. He had the only key and couldn't take off until everyone else had left. To get the employees to leave, he instructed them to mark their time cards to say they left at the regular time. Lee was fired shortly thereafter.

In her early forties, Lori described how she was terminated from her position as director of rehabilitation at a health system: "I had taken a vacation. When I came back, I went in a little early Monday morning to get organized before the others got there. As I pulled in, I saw my boss sitting on a picnic table. I spilled my pop and was rushing off to get inside to clean up. I said, 'What are you doing here?' She said, 'Can you follow me to the hospital?' I knew right then and there. I said, 'Can I go clean myself up? I spilled my pop.' She said, 'No, we have to leave now.' We got in our cars, and I followed her to our main building. For the two-mile drive across town, I was in shock. I couldn't believe what was happening. I knew I was being fired, but didn't know why.

"I was ushered into the hospital. We went to HR, and they said, 'We are terminating you.' 'On what grounds?' I asked. 'Failure to perform duties,' she said. 'You're kidding me. That can't be. You haven't followed any disciplinary option. You haven't counseled me. You haven't coached me.' They said, 'We were able to skip those steps.' I said, 'You haven't done a performance review, and it's been two years. All the ones before were excellent. How do I go from outstanding to terminated?'"

"You can sign this and get severance or not sign and forfeit," they told her. Lori didn't sign, saying, "I can't sign because it isn't true."

Also fired without due process was Wes, who had been with his organization fifteen years. "The guy I reported to was forced out. The guy who was my boss was no longer my boss. I now reported to the guy who was his foil. The two of them didn't get along. So now I worked for him. It went all right; things went fairly well.

"Before I was terminated, the company brought in a bunch of people from outside. They were on a fishing expedition to find something wrong. It seemed that they were suspicious of the operations head. They did an investigation. They talked to me and my team. I told my team to be cooperative, and we told them what we knew. We were doing a lot of other things as well, and I was involved in an acquisition, so I was busy.

"I knew I had not done anything improper. I felt secure and kept busy.

"They terminated the operations guy. He was out of town at the time. The first Monday in March at the end of the day, I got called to a conference room. Across from me were my boss and the owner's buddy. He handed me a letter. They explained there were things going on that I must have known about it, and I was terminated. They gave me a nasty letter saying that I wasn't getting any severance.

"I said, 'Give me some examples. What is your evidence of wrongdoing?' They said, 'It's none of your business—you're fired.'

"Maybe I was so busy I didn't see it coming. And I knew I had done nothing wrong."

It was common in this study for the interviewees not to have been given reasons for being let go. It was also typical for employers not to provide due process to an employee being accused. Employers do not have to give reasons for firing you. They do not have to justify or prove their allegations. Employment at will means it is simply the employer's decision whether or not to keep an employee.

This chapter introduced you to the stories of people who experienced firings, layoffs, and position eliminations. They describe a smattering of different experiences in what and how they were told. But this is just the beginning. These stories set the stage for the rest of this book. You'll read more about these job losses in the next chapter, where I investigate whether or not people had any hints or signals that they would be terminated.

## Key Takeaways

1. Understand the concept of employment at will and if it is enforced in your state.
2. Despite the commonly held notion of progressive discipline or fair notice, being fired often comes without warning.
3. It is unlikely that you will get a real description of why you were fired. Employment at will requires no reason or explanation.
4. Likewise, it is unlikely that you will be given the opportunity to explain or defend yourself. Employees aren't afforded due process in most situations.
5. Despite standard advice on how to fire someone, there is no single or uniform way people are terminated. (See "The Script on How to Fire Someone.")

## The Script on How to Fire Someone

Professional associations, journals, lawyers, and information technology, security, and human resource professionals have all provided advice to companies on how to fire people. One of our participants worked in human resources: "I have books on how to do it legally. From the human resources side, it's almost an art form. There's a script that should take no more than seven minutes. You'd better be light on your feet because you don't know what will happen."

Here is a summary of the key pieces of advice on how to fire people:

Preparation is typical prior to firing someone. The security team is often alerted so they can cancel building and parking access. The information services team is notified so they can cancel e-mail, software, and virtual private network access. The firing manager will typically work with someone in human resources to determine what if any severance, personal time off (PTO) payments, job-seeking assistance, or other support will be provided. In the case of large layoffs, this plan is choreographed to include a logistics plan for meeting with employee groups.

For individual terminations, the people doing the firing are often advised to schedule an appointment at the end of the day with the person being terminated. The goal is to have as few employees around to watch the person leave. It is usually recommended that someone accompany the firing manager as a witness or in case things get out of hand. The person doing the firing is encouraged to be direct and quick and not to sugarcoat things, discuss the reasons for termination, or allow the employee to think the termination is negotiable. Once told, the individual needs to have his or her work equipment retrieved: computer, phone, keys, name tag, and any other equipment. The company offers the individual a chance to come in on the weekend to retrieve his or her personal items or to have someone box his or her things and send them. Many companies choose to have the person leave immediately and even escort

26

them out the door. This helps prevent possible theft, strong emotional reactions after the shock wears off, and communication with current employees.

This is generic advice, and there is no shortage of it. Google "how to fire someone," and you will find multiple sources of information. Most cover these steps. Naturally, employers may vary in their practices and procedures, but this is generally what is advised for terminations that are not anticipated to be challenging or confrontational. Clearly, companies take greater precautions when an employee is suspected to be violent, under the influence, unstable, or disruptive.

# Ways to Communicate Involuntary Job Loss

| | |
|---|---|
| You're fired | We're having a reduction in workforce |
| You're being: | We're experiencing budget cuts |
| ...cut loose | You're no longer a fit |
| ...dismissed | You resigned |
| ...discharged | You retired |
| ...downsized | You are taking time off to spend with |
| ...forced to resign | family |
| ...laid off | You're not happy here |
| ...let go | We don't think this is working out |
| ...pink-slipped | We need a change |
| ...released | We're restructuring, reorganizing, con- |
| ...relieved | solidating, merging, acquiring |
| ...separated | Your division/program is being |
| ...terminated | eliminated |
| You're getting sacked | Your position is being outsourced |
| Your position is being | It's time we part ways |
| eliminated | We're taking a different direction |
| You got the axe | Your contract is not renewed |
| Your services are no lon- | It's time to move on |
| ger required | You don't have a future with this |
| | company |

# CHAPTER 2

## WHERE THERE'S SMOKE, THERE'S FIRE: SIGNS OF IMPENDING JOB LOSS

"We were traveling, and I got a bing for a meeting on
the last day of the month to meet with my boss. No
subject line—that should have been my first clue."
— MELISSA

T he interviewees talked extensively about job loss, its impact, and
their recovery. They also disclosed whether or not they had any
warning or noticed any signs of their impending job loss. I was
curious: Did they have an inkling they were being let go? Did they see it
coming, or were they completely surprised?

I asked these questions because in so many of my early conversations, I heard people claim they were completely blindsided by the termination. Yet as they reflected on the events that led up to their being
let go, several of them admitted that they wished they had paid attention
to the signals. This cognitive dissonance is understandable. Cognitive
dissonance is a term psychologists use to describe when people hold two
contradictory thoughts or beliefs or receive information that competes
with their existing belief system. This internal inconsistency is a source
of stress. If one believes he or she is doing a great job, that person has
no reason to suspect he or she will be fired. On the other hand, if those
pesky signs and signals that something is different appear, they may have
been disregarded or gone unnoticed. In retrospect, some people were
able to see the writing on the wall.

In general, the interviewees fell into two groups: those who were genuinely surprised and those who suspected they would lose their jobs. Often, being fired came as a complete surprise to people. Their stories had a similar pattern: they were praised and had great performance reviews, boasted strong accomplishments, and exhibited a great work ethic. They were shocked and completely unprepared for the event.

This seemed strange because most terminations are not impromptu. Nor are they solo events. It may be helpful to begin this chapter with a brief summary of what is typically involved in a termination or layoff. The reality is that most terminations are planned down to the how and when the person will be told. To build the case for firing someone, managers may reach out to others in the company to solicit feedback on how an employee is doing. Often a manager discusses the situation with human resources and his or her supervisor. Either as a genuine effort to help a person succeed or as an effort merely to demonstrate that the employer has done everything possible to make a person succeed, a manager may have offered one or more coaching sessions.

The act of firing itself requires coordination between the manager and at a minimum his or her manager, human resources, and possibly the legal department. Once the decision is made to terminate someone, the decision broadens to the IT department, which is on call to shut down the employee's e-mail, security clearances, and building and intranet access. Other key stakeholders will be notified so that work flow can be maintained. Suffice it to say, *prior to an employee's being terminated, a lot of people have been involved.*

In the cases of group layoffs or reductions in force, the plan is developed with the input and participation of even more people. And often the time frame to keep the layoffs confidential is longer than when just one person is being let go.

Despite all this, most interviewees claimed to have been blindsided. But with the benefit of twenty-twenty hindsight, they were able to look back and remember some of the signs indicating that their departure was inevitable. They also shared the results of their performance reviews. All the interviewees who were in their positions more than a year had been through a performance evaluation. Any other type of feedback they received about their job performance was also described.

As they looked back, they were able to identify changes or events that at the time did not seem threatening. Others admitted to noticing changes but dismissing them. They recognized that something wasn't quite right, but ignored it. This chapter will identify some of the signs and signals of an impending job loss as reported by the interviewees.

In other cases, interviewees were able to notice and interpret the warning signals. These individuals sensed that something was wrong and, as you will see in chapter 5, took steps to remove themselves before they were let go.

Here are their signs, starting with the most obvious and alarming one:

## Job Advertised or Posted

> "Did you put a blind ad in for my job?"
> —JEANNIE

When a company posts or advertises for a position while an incumbent is in place, it is an obvious sign that something is up. Business continuity is important, and sometimes companies begin recruiting for a replacement while someone currently occupies the position. But why would a company take the risk of the employee and coworkers finding out? Sometimes the incumbent is aware that a change is being made. The company has leveled with him or her and wants to work out a smooth transition. They may even have an arrangement for the employee to stay in the position until a certain time.

Some aren't so lucky, like Renee and Erica, whose stories are told in the previous chapter. Another example is Jeannie, a midlevel manager in a medium-size nonprofit. "I was working as a manager. We had been having difficulty meeting budget. But I was working on it. I was worried about my job, so I had been checking the job postings over the weekend. I found this one job; it sounded perfect. All the things I have experience in. Then I realized why it sounded great. It was exactly like my job, but there was no company listed. I went to human resources that Monday morning, and I was angry. 'Did you put a blind ad in for my job?' They hemmed and hawed and then called my boss, who finally admitted it. They had advertised for my job! I was furious; what an underhanded thing to do! So at that point, I knew I was out and did leave the company." Blind ads like the one Jeannie found serve to recruit for a position without identifying the company or the title of the individual who is being replaced.

While Jeannie was aware that her area was not meeting budget targets and that her position could be vulnerable, she was nonetheless shocked to see her job advertised.

## Offered a Demotion

Recruiting for a position currently occupied is a blatant sign that a job is in jeopardy. Being offered a demotion is another fairly obvious sign. A company does this for a variety of reasons: to move someone aside so that a new person can fill the position, to provide the company some breathing room while it works out a sticky or possibly litigious situation, to salvage a loyal or long-standing employee by giving them a position with less responsibility, and finally, to encourage a person to leave of his or her own accord instead of firing the person outright.

Here is Melissa's story: "I was in my office one day, and our human resources guy asked me if I wanted to go for a walk. I agreed, and as we were walking, he shared that a sales position had become available in one of our company's other divisions. He asked me if I would be interested in moving to that position. It was out of the blue. I was thinking, 'Oh my God.' Then he said, 'Since you're upset in your current position, would you be interested?' I said, 'I'm not upset. What do you mean?' He said, 'I heard you didn't like the new boss.' Now, I was a director. The position opening was a direct sales level job. I asked him, 'Why would I want to do that? What would make me go from a director back to a sales position? Would you do that?' He didn't answer. 'Seriously, I want to know your opinion, would you do that?' He said he wouldn't, but added, 'Seeing as you're upset.' I didn't take the bait. I said, 'I'm not upset.' He just hemmed and hawed and said he didn't know but thought he would mention it to me. That gave me the sensation that I wasn't long for the job. I knew something was up. I asked, 'Am I going to be fired?' He said, 'No, of course not; I just wanted to see if you were interested.' Looking back, I know that of course he knew more than he told me and that I was going to be fired."

Here is another example of someone being offered a demotion as a precursor to being fired. Paula shared how she was offered a demotion: "I was hired to be the number-two person in our department. After a year they offered me a demotion, a chance to work with organizational development. At that point, I was cut out of all the meetings. I wasn't in the know. I didn't have any direct reports. I didn't have enough to do. I went to my boss and told him I could handle more work and asked him for other assignments. He said he didn't have anything else for me to do. I saw the writing on the wall, so I began interviewing for other jobs."

Being offered a demotion is a sign that would give most people pause. No longer being in the know is another signal that your position could be in jeopardy. Paula recognized both signs.

If you are offered a demotion or have responsibilities taken away from you, it is likely an indicator that your employment is at risk. Demotions can serve to warn the employee, without stranding them without a job. Often companies think a demotion will be too difficult for the person to accept and hope the person will become motivated to look for employment elsewhere. Demotions also work to get someone out of the way so another person can be hired instead. The bottom line is that getting a demotion means the company does not see you as promotable or even capable of fulfilling the duties of your current position.

## Special Assignment

Similar to being offered a demotion is the "special assignment to the president" or "special projects" offer. To move a player out of the way, leaders may tap him or her to be on special assignment. This sounds like a prestigious position and in some cases it is. It can serve as a way to give a promising manager a view from the leader's office. But it's often a euphemism for moving someone out of a position to eventually fire him or her. When the special project is complete, the position can be eliminated or filled with a new hire.

This happened to Anna. She was running her own department when the boss asked her to take on a project for him. She was flattered that he asked and considered it a prestigious opportunity. And she genuinely liked him and wanted to help. She didn't realize that while she was on special assignment, her old position would be filled. Six months later she was fired.

The special projects role is typically used as a smooth way to transition someone out of a management role and into a position where he or she will have no direct reports. When the person ultimately is let go, there is less disruption in his or her former department. Often, by the time the person is let go, the company has had time to put a new supervisor in place. Unless the assignment as a special assistant or to a special project is treated as a regular job that you applied for, it is likely just a transition while the company eliminates your job or hires a replacement before letting you go.

After serving as a senior manager, Eve was moved out of that role to become the special assistant to the president. This allowed her to continue working for the company but shifted her away from the turbulence that resulted from a reduction in force. Eve was blamed for the jobs lost in her former department. Following this "promotion," over time more job duties were removed and assigned to others. She was then given the title "special projects." Eve read the writing on the corporate wall and found a new position.

In his article on the Wisebread website "You're Fired! 20 Signs That a Pink Slip Is Coming," Paul Michael writes: "What a cunning rouse [the following tactic] is. It's quite simple but efficient. In your old position, it may have been very difficult or almost impossible to get rid of you. But if the company promotes you into a newly created role, with less responsibility and no direct reports, then you have a new scenario...position elimination. It's hard to fire someone. It's easy to eliminate a position. You can get rid of anyone, even protected classes (older folks, pregnant ladies, etc.), if you simply eliminate a position. So, be afraid. Be very afraid. If you were formerly 'Account Manager' and are now 'Director in Charge of Special Project Development,' you may as well clear out your desk right now."

## Financial Difficulties

If the company is experiencing financial distress, it could be a tip-off that you could be let go. Aware of the financial challenges in her organization, Lesley made plans to exit. "They were eroding their reserve. They sold some assets. I watched them blow through that money in five years. So much expense creep. I started to figure out that when it was time for cuts, I would be one of them. I wouldn't be sheltered by my boss. They never accepted me, but I took a lot of work off them. That made me decide the time was right."

Joe was integral to the team that planned the layoffs in his organization. "We decided that we had to eliminate sixty positions, including management. The boss asked for a revitalized management structure. We knew we were making cuts. There were teams to work on it. With the elimination of senior leadership and management, we were going to make outplacement services available. I met with a labor attorney to discuss severance for those being laid off. I assumed the organization would take care of me." Joe had no inkling that he would be next. Soon after, Joe learned he would be included in the reduction in force he was in charge of planning, communicating, and implementing.

## Gallows Humor

"I hope you quit and get a new job,
so I don't have to fire you."
—MARK'S BOSS

As mentioned earlier, most firings are not spontaneous decisions. It takes time to process the decision between the manager and human resources. Often other departments are also involved. And while the information is supposed to be confidential, the circle of those in the know grows larger. As time passes, more and more people walk uneasily around the workplace knowing that someone is going to be fired. This can sometimes last for weeks, even months.

This was Mark's experience with gallows humor: "I was new in a position, recruited by a competitor of my former company. They really made me feel wanted, like my expertise was really needed. My new supervisor provided me with some initial goals. I let him know that all the things he wanted for the organization were doable; I would just need more time than what he proposed. Well, a few months into the job, my boss and I met to talk about my progress. Most of the areas made great progress, but one area was not where we wanted it to be. He joked, 'I hope you quit and get a new job, so I don't have to fire you.' I was making so much progress I didn't take him seriously. A couple months later I was out of a job."

Here is another story involving gallows humor. Nick's boss was let go and an interim person was named. "Another sign I missed—I walked into a room where a new leader was meeting with my former boss's team. I walked in and he said, 'As bad as I feel, at least I'm not you!' I thought he was joking. I just laughed and sat down. He wasn't joking; he knew I was going to be let go."

These are two good examples of humor that isn't funny. Both supervisors appeared to know something about the future of their employees. They used gallows humor to express themselves, but because the message was cloaked in humor, it was not received.

## Are You Still Here?

> "Are you leaving? I really hate to see you
> go. I am so sad that you are leaving us. I
> really respect you as a professional. They are
> throwing the baby out with the bathwater."
> —A MEMBER OF JANICE'S UPPER MANAGEMENT TEAM

The notion that numerous people are aware when someone is about to lose their job has played out in the news. For example, when David Gregory was the moderator of NBC's *Meet the Press,* there were rumors and speculation that he was going to be fired. The talk was so prevalent that Mike Wallace, a former moderator of *Meet the Press,* said NBC was mistreating his fellow Sunday morning show host. "We all understand we don't have a right to these jobs," Wallace said on Fox News' *MediaBuzz*. "It's a tremendous privilege. On the other hand, I think we do have a right to be treated properly and not shabbily. And if you're going to get rid of David Gregory—and I don't know that they are, I have no inside information—then they ought to just do it. But this kind of twisting in the wind…it's unseemly." He added, "They ought to either say, 'He's our guy, and we're sticking with him,' or they should get rid of him. But they shouldn't put him in this limbo."

The speculation was true, and David Gregory was fired as the moderator of *Meet the Press* in 2013. As mentioned earlier, prior to an actual firing, many people have been advised, consulted, and involved. And word gets out.

Here are more examples that build on the theme that many people know about a pending termination before it is executed. Going to work as usual, three people interacted with coworkers who were surprised that they were *still* at work. Mark worked in one of his company's branches. "Two weeks before I was let go, I spent a day at our company's regional headquarters. Nothing unusual, just a couple of meetings. I saw one of the directors in the hallway and stopped to say hi. He said, 'Are you still here? I thought you had left.' He looked aghast. He was obviously a part of the conversation that my time was done. But I wasn't aware of it. At the time, I didn't think anything of it. I was business as usual. I told my wife, 'Something's up.' Two weeks later I was fired."

Notice the cognitive dissonance in Mark's words as he describes what happened. He said that at the time he didn't think anything of it, but right afterward he told his wife that something was up. This is a common theme among the people interviewed. On the one hand they noticed the disconnect, but on the other hand, they ignored it.

Janice, who had fifteen years of service with her company, also heard of her impending firing through a coworker. She recounted her story: "I stopped into my office to see my assistant on my way to a conference. I had a coat, my laptop, and a briefcase—I was loaded down. After seeing my assistant, I headed back to the car. On the way a coworker in another department stopped me and said, 'Are you leaving? I really hate to see you go. I am so sad that you are leaving us. I really respect you as a professional. They are throwing the baby out with the bathwater.' I told her I was only leaving for a conference and had to get on the road. I thought something was up after that."

In case you think this is unusual, here's yet another person who heard about her demise from a coworker: "One of my coworkers was called by his boss's boss. She told him I was leaving. He then walked over to my office and told me what she said. Then, I got an e-mail with no subject line saying I had a meeting at four o'clock. I thought I was going to be fired, so I prepared my letter of resignation."

## Family and Friends Warn You

> "The handwriting is on the wall."
> —JOE'S WIFE

Sometimes the employee's family and friends are able to recognize the warning signs before they do. While Joe believed he would be shielded from the cuts in his organization, his wife was less confident. "She was telling me all along to look for another job. She said, 'The handwriting is on the wall.' She knew I didn't get along with my boss. She was right."

Lesley spoke of several encounters with colleagues who tried to warn her: "You need to get out." "You're too good for this place." "Don't let them pull you down." She shared a story of confiding her concerns to a colleague, "I remember one night I went out on a limb and went to his office and asked him something. 'Do you know how HR is treating me?' He said, 'I do.' I asked, 'Why is it being allowed?' He said, 'I adore you, but I can't jeopardize my job for you. My advice is you need to get out. As long as she is in HR, you will not get promoted. She will find a way to fire you. A policy. Anything.'" Her husband agreed, saying, "Get the hell out of that place." Lesley eventually heeded their advice and planned her exit.

"My husband kept saying, 'I don't trust her. You need to be careful,' referring to the person who ultimately initiated Mona's firing. Mona shared that she was convinced that her husband was just cynical and became friends with the coworker. "I should have listened to my husband, and really, if I'm honest, to that little voice inside of me."

## Meetings Canceled, Contact Avoided

Again, remember that firing someone is a team effort. Several people will know about the impending separation before the individual knows. So all these people are now in the uncomfortable situation of knowing someone is about to be fired. They have three choices when it comes to interacting with this employee: joke about it, act like nothing is wrong, or avoid the person.

Avoidance is generally easier than the uncomfortable act of facing someone about to be fired. Standard meetings may be canceled if the person about to be fired is scheduled to be there. E-mails will cease. Coworkers' eyes will dart away. This happens for several reasons. One, the person may worry that his or her interaction will somehow be seen by the employee as different in some way and raise red flags. Two, by avoiding the person, the person will not have to pretend that it's business as usual and risk being accused by the person of lying to or deceiving him or her. Three, often those in the know understandably feel sympathy for the person about to be let go and find it difficult to face the person.

Looking back, Alexa could identify avoidance as one of the signs she was about to lose her job. "Leading up to this, I had been told I didn't have to be in meetings anymore. So that was like a week before. I had been reserving rooms for the team, and then they said I didn't need to be there 'because the space was so cramped.' They didn't say they didn't want me. They used an excuse that the meeting room was too small to be there. I didn't question it as much as I should have. Honestly, the only other thing was my supervisor pushed back my meeting for three weeks. She didn't want to meet with me. We had only one call."

Julie, a frontline manager in her early thirties, remembered how her manager, who was also her friend, acted. "I was off sick on Friday. On Monday it was weird; my boss didn't do her usual check-in. She didn't call to ask how I was feeling. She didn't call to talk about the week ahead. That was normal for us. We were friends, and we always checked in on each other." Julie was let go that week.

A senior-level manager in the hospitality industry, Karen shared how her coworkers started avoiding her: "I didn't think much of it at the time. I remember this so clearly. I was at my desk, and one of the HR managers was in the area. He stopped to chat with the person who sat directly in front of me. They weren't talking work, they were just having friendly chit-chat. As he looked up to leave, he caught my eye and looked down, turned around, and left. Total avoidance. I thought, 'Wow, he looked right at me and didn't even say hi.' At the time I thought it was weird; I thought maybe he just didn't like me. Now I see he was avoiding me. He was there when I was told my position was eliminated.

"The week before I was let go, several of my meetings were canceled or removed from my calendar. Looking back, I can see that was intentional. I was surprised because one of the events on my schedule was a celebration dinner to mark a milestone accomplishment in my department and the other was an invitation to the boss's Christmas party. I was let go the day of our celebration, so I didn't get to attend. And obviously I didn't go to the boss's holiday party."

It's awkward, uncomfortable, and even disheartening to work with someone when you know he or she is about to be let go. So, many employees cope by avoidance.

Janice noticed a big change in the way people treated her. "Prior to that, I had participated in leadership meetings. Now I wasn't included. Now I couldn't give information to the leaders about what was going on. Abruptly, those kinds of inclusion stopped when the new leader was brought in. They had their own group meeting. No communication in or out of the meeting. There was a window in the meeting room where they met. They put up blinds so no one could see in. They became very secretive. Who knows what they were cooking up?" Janice was encouraged to leave her position shortly thereafter. Being excluded from meetings you were previously a part of is another form of avoidance.

In addition to being subjected to gallows humor, Nick described how others avoided him, even someone he considered a friend. "I came down a hallway and saw a friend coming out of the elevator. I waved and said hi. He just avoided eye contact with me and walked away."

Gail was let go after fifteen years as a senior leader with her company. "I came into work while on maternity leave. I was so excited to take my new baby into work and show her to my coworkers. I took the baby to see my boss and my co-worker, Candy. She was also a mother and had a family of her own. It was weird. She didn't even touch my baby. Most women are excited by a new baby. She was very cool. I didn't think anything of it then, but in hindsight, I see she was in on my being fired. The day I came back from maternity leave, I was fired."

## You Blew the Whistle

> "I figured she would be pissed, but I
> didn't think she could fire me."
> —BRENDA

A computer specialist, Lee started work at a new company in what seemed to be a job that was a perfect fit for him. The culture of the office was a bit unfiltered, but Lee claims he tried to roll with it. "I became upset when I saw the office assistant having to endure all these inappropriate jokes, loud outbursts, and screaming. It just seemed to be the way it was there. But then one guy, a real bully, started making jokes at other people's and other people's wives' expense. I let him know I didn't appreciate it, but that only escalated his rudeness. So I went to HR. I told them about his offensive behavior and how he was especially offensive to the female employees. The HR director was fidgeting; you could tell he didn't want to hear this. He didn't want to take this guy on. But he thanked me for reporting this. I don't think others shared his point of view. At the Christmas party, I met up with the branch manager in the buffet line. He looked at me like, "Why are you eating my hamburgers?" I could tell he was angry at me. Within a month I was fired. Well, they said they were cutting my position. It was like the branch manager was thinking I was trying to hurt his company."

Pete shared his story of challenging the office culture at an insurance company: "I wanted to make sure the patients got what they needed. But the company was all about the money. I couldn't deny people the care they needed. They wanted me to control costs by not approving needed services. I was fired because they wanted me to do unethical things and I wouldn't do them."

Similarly, Sam experienced a backlash from reporting an issue. "There was an issue that we all agreed had to be solved. It wasn't a secret; everyone was aware. It kept getting put off because it would mean the company had to spend some money. I talked to legal and to HR. It was time to get it resolved. That was the end for me. I was let go soon after."

An ethical issue cost Brenda her job. "I knew it was coming, because I totally disagreed with my boss. At one point, I dug in. It was an ethics issue. I figured she would be pissed, but I didn't think she could fire me. I was living in an employment-at-will state. I said no to something. To this day I know I did the right thing ethically. She had signed a contract that committed us to a lot. We beat three national companies. We got it, and everyone was excited. The next day, a Thursday, she said, 'You need to let them know we can't fulfill the contract.' I told her we can't do that. She said, 'We just can't.' I pleaded with her, 'You just signed in good faith.' She insisted that I call them. I said no."

Brenda's performance evaluation was on the calendar for the following week. Instead of a performance review, her boss came into her office that morning and fired her. Brenda asked for the reasons she was being fired. Her boss told her, "It's no longer a good fit." She was escorted out of the building and told to could come in Saturday with HR and clean out her office.

As a senior sales manager in home improvement, Brent became concerned about some of the human resources practices in his organization. Not getting anywhere through normal channels of communication, he became a whistle-blower. Even though he and his team had the best sales performance in the company, he was fired.

Gail also experienced retribution as a result of questioning the judgment of a co-worker. In a meeting she challenged her colleague's desire to hire a consulting firm while the company was having financial difficulties. "As soon as I raised my voice about spending that money and the way it was done without the group endorsement, it smelled. There is a part of me that knew as soon as I did that I was done."

Joe also experienced the consequences of "telling truth to power." His organization was facing insurance payment reductions and had to reduce its expenses by millions. He and the CFO believed that their patriarchal, "management by objective" (MBO) management style had to go and a different management approach was needed. Joe, the CFO, and several senior leaders attended a leadership development seminar based on the quality management culture-change style of organizational leadership.

Joe said, "Coming out of that, a major education and transformation session occurred. I was elected by my peers to lead the effort to get a more participative, collaborative leadership team. As that work with my team of colleagues proceeded, it became apparent that the CEO was not totally engaged in this work, even though he said he was. His actions and words didn't match. We talked among our group about how to approach him about changing his management style. I convened a meeting with the CEO to discuss his style. That meeting did not go well. He verbalized appreciation, but outside of the meeting he made it known he was upset that he was confronted."

The CEO found a performance improvement initiative he was more comfortable with and abandoned the work Joe and several senior leaders initiated. When it came time to make the expense cuts, Joe's position was included.

Many organizations have compliance programs that encourage employees to report ethical or legal problems. Many even have nonretaliation policies to protect them. However, these whistle-blowers didn't fare well in their organizations, and that's not unusual. Despite the rhetoric and encouragement to report ethical issues, some companies may be threatened by employees who blow the whistle. In the *Fraud* magazine article "Be Prepared Before You Blow the Whistle," Patricia A. Patrick warns that most whistle-blowers get fired. "Seventy-four percent of the whistle-blowers in my review were terminated. Another 6 percent were suspended and 5 percent were transferred against their wishes. The remaining 15 percent were given poor evaluations, demoted or harassed."

## Crabs in a Bucket

"I was in total shock. I haven't ever been told that. I am
an overachiever; I thought that was a good thing."
—LESLEY

The saying "crabs in a bucket" refers to a phenomenon where people pull one another down rather than celebrate their success. When a crab is placed in a bucket, it will try to climb out and escape. If a few crabs are placed in a bucket, and one tries to climb out, the rest of the crabs pull it down by the legs and try to escape themselves. Like crabs in a bucket, sometimes coworkers, including those in leadership positions, try to pull down high achievers, even though a high achiever should be considered an asset to the company.

Lesley found out the hard way how colleagues resented her achievements. "So I came on board in a new position to help oversee and develop a new product line. But I had no idea at the time what animosity it would create. It's hard to believe, but I was at work at six o'clock at night and thought I was alone. A corporate HR person came into my office and shut my door. She said to me, 'You're on thin ice in this organization. You are making everyone else look bad.' Basically, I am doing well, getting things done better than the others. 'If you don't slow down and get with the pace and the culture, you will not be with the organization long. And if you tell our supervisor about this, I will deny everything. And who do you think he will believe?'

"I was in total shock. I haven't ever been told that. I am an overachiever; I thought that was a good thing. To literally be told if I said anything, she would deny it. It's like the movies—but I never expected it in real life. It bothered me so badly. I was carrying a box of supplies downstairs on my way out and fell down an entire flight of stairs. I hit my head and blacked out. I managed to get up and drive home. I wouldn't dare tell anyone I was injured. I couldn't dare report a worker's comp claim."

## Micromanaging

> "It's tough. I had to ask for my work each morning."
> —SONDRA

According to several interviewees, being micromanaged may be another sign that your job is on the line. It can also cause you to begin to doubt your abilities and to lose confidence, which in turn can affect your ability to do a good job.

Sondra, a recent college graduate, shared several times in her interview that she was micromanaged. "It's tough. I had to ask for my work each morning." Sondra believed her boss didn't trust her to do her job well.

During his years at his organization, Bruce had several different supervisors. But he realized things were not going well with his newest one. "I did see it coming. I knew it was inevitable. I don't know if it was self-fulfilling prophecy. It was like someone was looking at your work through a microscope or had a target on your back. Every move you make, you're second-guessing yourself. You aren't confident. You are doing things you don't normally do. It tripped me up all the time, this second-guessing, and the fact that there was someone looking over my shoulder.

"I was used to bosses who had confidence in my ability. With my new boss, I don't believe he had confidence in me. He wanted to be sure every 'i' was dotted, every 't' crossed. He wanted everything in detail. I said it was micromanaging. That was not his perception. This led to a more tense relationship with a supervisor than I was accustomed to. Bruce was let go abruptly.

As a project manager in the energy field, Don shared how his boss became more involved. After Don took the initiative to develop internal systems and processes, his manager started micromanaging. "I took the confusing things and made my own spreadsheets, organizing many things others had only wrestled with. I made a system for doing our work. My department manager felt this was a waste of time and began zeroing in on me. He set up a series of weekly meetings and began mentoring me. I felt incredibly intimidated, as if I were under the microscope."

## Performance Improvement Plans

Most organizations have in place the practice of conducting annual employee evaluations. This is one method organizations use to document that they provided an employee with feedback as to how his or her performance needed to improve. The feedback comments may be limited to the performance evaluation form. But if the company believes it is serious, they may give the employee a formal performance improvement plan or action plan. If you get repeated coaching from your supervisor or are placed on a performance action plan, take it seriously. This is a clear sign that your job is in jeopardy.

Bruce, who earlier talked about being micromanaged, shared his experience with performance reviews: "My anniversary was that October. No celebration or anything. What I did have was an evaluation in November, and that was the first negative evaluation I ever had. I felt the writing was on the wall. I'm not used to having a bad review. I even told another employee, the finance person, there are some things we needed to do in case I got let go.

"And at home I told my wife, 'There's a good chance I could get let go.' We owned some investment properties. We needed to sell them off. 'Let's prepare for the worst and hope for the best.' We did sell our properties, and I was let go." Bruce wisely saw the signs and began making preparations in case his hunch came true.

Don described his challenge in meeting his boss's expectations after he was put on a performance improvement plan. "My manager would sit in his darkened office and shout at me from across the hall, barking orders. This didn't faze me; I had worked overseas and had seen much worse. The woman in my neighboring office confided that she had been in the same predicament with him years ago and that she brought a harassment claim against him, which saved her job."

As mentioned earlier, Don then went through some intense exams that his manager and department manager had devised for him to prove his skills, which he had to work on in addition to his already heavy workload.

He described the stress he was under and the ordeal of the exams: "My office was like that of a college professor. It had a huge oak door, and early on I had taken to closing the door and praying or reading the Bible during lunch. Now I literally closed the door and got face down on the floor before God begging Him to save my job and provide peace through this stressful time. I had the Lord's perfect peace (yes, I worried, but it somehow seemed as if it would all work out).

"While working on the exam, I could ask questions, but they had to be formal. During one of these Q&A sessions, I sensed all the answers were leading to the fact that the problem they gave me had no solution. They were so proud of this fact—a Star Trek test. It was so evident. That night I thought, "OK, so here is a problem without a solution. What would be your second choice, your backup plan?" I finished this take at a solution. When the day came to present my solution, their disappointment and surprise that I had realized this was only too evident. They left my office satisfied with my solution but promised there would be another test next week—and this one would be tough. I feared what was next if I had just solved the problem without a solution.

"The next exam came, and I feverishly worked on it, yet my solution was costly and cumbersome. I was running out of time and energy. They had asked for a nice PowerPoint presentation of my solution, but when the day came, I had literally run out of time and only had pencil flow diagrams for portions of the solution. They smiled and were almost giddy upon leaving my office."

Being given an impossible task is one way a company can construct a reason to fire someone. In his Wisebread article, Paul Michael explains this tactic: "The company may need a big reason to give you the boot, especially if you've done everything right and are the life and soul of your department. Enter the impossible task. If you've been given a thankless task, at least be thankful for the blatant tipoff that you're about to be let go."

## Leadership Transition

> "A new leader was appointed. I just knew
> he wanted to pick his own team."
> —ASHLEY

By far, the biggest sign of impending job loss from the people inter-viewed for this book is getting a new boss. *More than half* of them expe-rienced a change in their direct supervisors shortly before they were terminated. Here are a few examples:

An attorney at a law firm, Connie was caught in the web of a lead-ership transition. "As soon as he became my supervisor, I knew I was doomed. Everyone told him they wanted to work with me. All the clients requested me, not him. I was doomed. I would have been miserable if I had stayed. I later saw the writing on the wall. He kept three of the twenty-four departments. I had twenty departments. Another person had one. He gave me the problem areas. The writing was on the wall. I see that now."

Ashley took a job with a new organization after experiencing some conflicts in her former company. "Beth, a longtime colleague, called me and asked me to work for her. She was very persistent. I had a job I loved, but there were some conflicts within my organization. She kept at it and was persuasive, so eventually I agreed to leave my job and work for her. It was a promotion too, and in a great organization. I enjoyed my work and was very happy to be working with her.

"Then Beth suddenly announced her retirement. She had an affair with someone at work and had to resign. I said, 'Beth, how could you do this to me? How could you bring me here and now you're leaving?' I wanted to stay.

"A new leader was appointed. I just knew he wanted to pick his own team. We agreed to say it was a restructure. I felt so terrible I just wanted to hide. I was ashamed. I couldn't talk to anyone. I didn't know if anyone would even want to talk to me."

After twenty-eight years with a local human services agency, Diane was let go. "A new executive director was hired. At first things were going well. He liked me, I liked him. He promoted me to director. In a month or so, things had turned and he looked for reasons to get rid of me.

"In hindsight he let go of everyone from my era, except for one man. He wanted to get rid of me to find a way to hire his pet friend from his old job. One way to pay for her was to get rid of me. I learned this later."

After fifteen years with a major institution, Nick was asked to leave his position. "There were telltale signs, but I didn't see them. I remember an appointment with the president suddenly appeared on my boss's calendar. I asked him what it was; he said he didn't know. When he came back from the appointment, he was in shambles. He was fired. I didn't think it would affect me at all, even if my job was eliminated. I really thought I could add value to the company. I had done so many jobs there."

Brenda recalled the first time she was fired: "I didn't see it coming. I was in total shock. I walked around the office and said, 'I was just fired.' It was a deal between my boss and her boss. My boss was new in her job. I had sixteen years in this field; she had four months. I was trying to help her and make her look good. She would say the craziest things. It was threatening for her. She shouldn't have been hired."

An engineer with sixteen years of service at his company, Andrew reported how his position was eliminated in a downsizing after new leadership was brought in. "Two vice presidents were hired right before I was terminated, and then right after, eight new directors were hired from outside the organization—all at a level below where I was at. The two new VPs wanted their own people in there, so they got rid of the old."

Renee's troubles started when she got a new boss, who was recruited from outside the company. Her new boss posted an ad for her position and told her she had to reapply for her job. Renee said, "I figured, she wants to look around, looking to see what's out there, what she can get. And I may or may not be what she wants."

A leadership transition in her company led to Melissa being fired. "The person they hired was completely looney tunes. She never met with any staff and met with me twice in four months. And she didn't know anything about our industry. She wanted us to focus on one area to the exclusion of others. I guess that's something that should have set off alarm bells."

## Your Rival Got the Job

When positions open up, most companies have a policy of posting them internally first, before the jobs are externally advertised. If two colleagues are applying for the same job, the person not selected could be at risk. For instance, Hannah and Ben applied for the same senior leadership position in their company. They had worked together but often didn't see eye to eye. Hannah was selected, and the outgoing leader then fired Ben. As Hannah put it, "He knew it would be difficult for me to have to deal with Ben. He wanted me to have a strong start."

Recall Joe, who was a senior leader in health care. He recruited Ellen to work at the company, and he felt they worked well together. Their boss left and the two of them competed for her job. Ellen got the job, and one of her first moves was to fire Joe. Internal politics can be brutal.

## Friday, 4:00 p.m. Meeting—No Subject Line

"No subject line—that should have been my first clue."
—MELISSA

After being fired from her job, Gail found work at a company where she stayed for several years. She was aware that new leadership would be coming into her organization and was hoping she would have the opportunity to continue in her role.

"One Thursday I got an e-mail from my boss asking me to meet him at 4:00 p.m. on Friday. I met a friend for lunch. I told her I thought I was about to be fired. I didn't see any other reason why my boss would need to meet with me. So I called in sick on Friday and got myself ready in case this was going to happen. I went back to work on Monday and it didn't happen. Weeks went by and nothing. Then the new boss came. He said they didn't need my position anymore. So I think I was right; they just decided to fire me after the new boss came."

Melissa described her experience: "I was traveling with a colleague, and I got an e-mail from my boss requesting a meeting for the last day of the month. No subject line—that should have been my first clue. I looked over at my colleague and said, 'I think they are going to let me go on Monday.' I was looking on the company e-mail system calendar to see who had a busy schedule, and I saw the HR director was busy at that time. But then I was thinking, 'They can't just let me go. We are profitable. Who lets a profit center go?' So I was in the office early for the 8:00 a.m. meeting. I was there first. They were dumbfounded when they walked in and I was already there. Seeing HR there with my boss, I knew I was done for."

## You Took Sick Leave

Being away on medical leave might make you feel secure in your job. After all, who fires someone on medical leave? However, when you are away from the office, it gives your boss the opportunity to check up on you, to see how others think you're doing. If they all decide to let you go, your absence helps them work out the details of the termination with human resources, information technology, and others.

Four of our interviewees were let go in the time surrounding a medical leave. Gail spoke taking family leave to have a baby. She described how her colleagues were reticent around her when she brought her baby to the office. On her first day back to work, Gail was fired.

While on medical leave getting rehab after her knee surgery, Connie received a certified letter saying she was no longer employed. The courier delivered the notice to the outpatient therapy center where she was being treated.

A breast cancer survivor, Diane had worked at her company for twenty-eight years. The Friday afternoon before she was to go on medical leave for breast reconstruction surgery, she was fired. Not only did she have to worry about the surgery and her recovery, she had to worry about how she would support her family.

Susan was on medical leave from her job as a branch manager in a large national company. When she recovered and was well enough to return to work, she asked to be placed in the metropolitan area where she lived, which had dozens of branches. The headquarters refused to place her in her area and offered her only small, rural branches far from home.

It is a lot easier to plan for someone's termination or de facto termination while he or she is out of the office.

## Sometimes It's Obvious from Day 1

> "Don't sit there—anyone who sits there gets fired."
> —LEE'S NEW COWORKER

It may seem odd, but for some of my interviewees, there were clues early on, before their work was even known to the company. For Brenda, it was that little voice inside her that told her the job wouldn't last. Brenda remembered how she left the third time she was fired. "My boss said, 'I will give you a couple hours to pick up your belongings.' I said, 'It won't take me long to pick up a coffee cup.' I never brought anything personal to that office. I knew from day one it was short term." Brenda's gut feeling was right. Later she learned from a board member that she had lasted the longest of anyone in the position.

Lee shared his first clue that he was not long for his organization, a technology company. "My first day at work should have been a sign. I walked into the office, and my boss said, 'Sit anywhere you want,' pointing to a group of desks. I picked one out and walked to it. One of my coworkers said, 'Don't sit there—anyone who sits there gets fired.'" Lee's coworkers knew the culture of their organization and used humor to get their point across to Lee. Lee was let go from his job one year after he started.

Soon after he started his new position, Mark noticed a pattern in his new company. Firings were common. "They were not open. Then I realized that's their M.O. They hire people, then chew them up, and spit them out. They fired the person I replaced. They said she left to take care of her mother, but her mother had passed away before she left. I met her at a workshop once." Recall that Mark lasted one year in his new position.

Karen recounted her experience at a new position: "I got hired for this great new job and showed up to work on my first day. The person I was replacing was still there. My boss explained that the company needed some things done and contracted with her for certain jobs after they let her go. So I met the person I was replacing. She looked a little like me. And from the sound of things, she had a strong personality. I have been told I do as well. So over the next few weeks, I got to know her and her work, and she did some really good stuff. And that's when I knew—if they fired this woman, I probably wouldn't last long here either. Well, I made it four years, so longer than I thought I would."

If there has been a string of firings before you, or you learn that no one in the position has lasted more than a year, it's a signal the company may have internal issues that are not resolved. Or if a seemingly capable person had the job before you and was let go, it could be a sign that the company is not poised with successful leadership. It is a good idea during the interview process to ask what happened to the person who previously held the job.

## You Started a New Job

This is a tough one to chew, but starting a new job can actually be a risk factor in losing a job. A study by Leadership IQ, a global leadership training and research company, reports that a staggering 46 percent of new hires fail within the first eighteen months on the job. The three-year research project studied 5,247 hiring managers from 312 public, private, business, and health-care organizations. Together these managers hired more than twenty thousand employees during the study period. The managers were asked to give reasons why their new hires didn't work out. And it wasn't only because they weren't qualified or competent. The study revealed the following top reasons why new hires fail:

- Motivation: Employees did not have the passion or the desire to excel on the job.
- Coachability: Employees could not understand or incorporate feedback from management or coworkers.

- Technical Capabilities: Employees did not possess the technical or functional skills to perform the job.
- Emotional Intelligence: Employees lacked self-awareness and could not control their own emotions or assess those of others.
- Temperament: Employees did not fit into company culture and did not have the right personality or attitude.

A common buzz phrase used to fire people is, "You're not a fit." The Leadership IQ study confirms that four of the five top reasons people are fired within eighteen months of starting a new job relate to "fit." Perceived lack of emotional intelligence, coachability, temperament, and motivation were most commonly cited as reasons for new hires being fired, far outweighing deficits in technical or functional skills. In fact, only 11 percent of employees in this study were let go because they lacked necessary skills. The other 89 percent were fired due to personality factors.

The employee is typically blamed for lacking emotional intelligence or not fitting in. But in several of my interviews, it was the employee's coworkers who took the initiative to exclude or demean them. For example, Alexa recalls feeling like she didn't fit in with her new team. "They lied to me and tried to make me feel as small and as inept as possible. The people didn't want to get to know me. Whenever there was banter, I felt I had to be silent. I wasn't a part of things. I was excluded from the team." Likewise, Lesley said of her coworkers, "I was excluded from the team. They never accepted me."

## Key Takeaways

Although some are more overt than others, there are usually signs that someone is about to be fired. *Pay attention to patterns of interaction and communication.*

1. If you suspect you are being let go, avoid taking a meeting the last week of the month. Employers must pay out health care through the end of the month you are terminated.

2. A new supervisor is cause for concern: more than half of the people interviewed for this study were let go by a new supervisor.
3. If you get a new supervisor, do your best to focus on how he or she wants things done, not how things used to get done.
4. If you take a new job, be prepared. Nearly half of all new hires fail within the first eighteen months.

# CHAPTER 3

## YOU'RE NOT FIREPROOF: NO ONE IS SAFE FROM GETTING FIRED

In the preceding chapter, the interviewees explained how they saw signs of their impending termination—if not in real time, in hindsight. They registered the sign as something out of the ordinary, but in real time, didn't typically understand what it meant. These are signs that all of us can look out for in our own positions.

A common thread among the interviews was that they saw themselves as dedicated, hardworking employees. In fact, most of them were validated through praise, promotion, or even awards. They thought they were fireproof. They could not insulate themselves from being let go.

We're all taught that if you work hard, do a good job, and stay loyal, you will be rewarded. And our interviewees were no different—they all embraced the same lesson. This chapter highlights why the interviewees felt safe and secure in their jobs—indeed, fireproof. Like them, you may be tempted to think that if you do a great job and the company is doing well, your job is safe. But that is not necessarily the case.

Moreover, it is natural to think your job is safe if you have been in a company for many years, or had strong performance reviews, or were recently promoted. The interviewees certainly learned differently.

It came up in my interviews time and time again: *People were fired who truly thought they were an asset to their companies and believed their companies recognized it.* That's a big disconnect. Their perception of

56

their own value was not what their companies asserted when they were let go.

This chapter looks at what specifically led people to feel comfortable with job security. Here are some reasons why most of us might feel we are not vulnerable to losing our jobs and the actual experiences of our respondents.

## Years of Service

> "Twenty-eight years. I started when I was twenty-one working part time in the home to pay my way through college. I did direct care on weekends, then graduated and was promoted to run a group home. Then I was promoted to manager and was running five sites. I met my husband there."
> —DIANE

Tenure in an organization is typically thought to be a good thing. It's understandable that people who have worked in the same organization for, let's say, more than five years, anticipate having their employment continued. In the case of layoffs or reduction in workforce, tenure with an organization is often used to decide who stays. But long-standing tenure in an organization does not guarantee job security. More than half of our respondents lost their job after serving more than five years with the company.

- Bruce: "I had been there over ten years."
- Andrew: "I officially had sixteen years of service with the same company."
- Melissa: "I had been with the company five-plus years."
- Connie: "I worked for twenty-eight years as an attorney in a law firm. I rose through the ranks, beginning there soon after law school, to a high-level position in the firm."
- Diane: "Twenty-eight years. I started when I was twenty-one working part time in a home to pay my way through college. I did

direct care on weekends, then graduated and was promoted to run a group home. Then I was promoted to manager and was running five homes. I met my husband there."

- Janice: "Fifteen years there."
- Elizabeth: "Thirteen years."
- Nick: "I served fifteen years with my organization."
- Renee: "Twenty-seven years."
- Julie: "Seven years."
- Wes: "Twenty years."
- Lori: "I worked there seventeen years."
- Gail: "I worked there for fifteen years."

No need to belabor the point further. According to the experiences of the interviewees, long-standing tenure in an organization does not insulate one from the possibility of being fired. Joe, who was let go after sixteen years with his health-care organization, cautions, "Longevity in an organization can blind you."

## Good Connections

> "I thought that gave me some protection."
>
> —JOE

Joe was part of a team of managers who had to process millions of dollars in cuts in the organization. Despite the fact that cuts were imminent, Joe thought he was fireproof because of his relationships and connections. "I thought I would survive. I assumed that because of my strong relationship with the CFO and my leadership work, the organization would take care of me. And my wife was the daughter of a top physician, so I thought that gave me some protection. I was tied to the community." Joe learned that the layoffs he was part of planning and implementing now included him. "I was not savvy enough or mature enough at the time to know I was vulnerable, and I did not take definitive action to provide for myself and my family."

## Great Performance Reviews

"How do I go from outstanding to terminated?"
—LORI

Performance reviews or annual evaluations provide companies with a formal process for assessing their employees. Typically a performance review includes a review of the individual's job skills, accomplishments, and areas for improvement. Many companies will tie in pay increases to the employee's performance review.

I wondered if any of the people interviewed were warned through a performance review that they needed to improve. Were any of them given warning that their performance was not up to par? Did they get any specific feedback?

The responses fell in one of two categories: people who had all positive performance reviews, and those who had all positive performance reviews *until their current supervisor.*

Here is a sampling from the first group, those with all positive reviews:

- "All my evaluations were 'exceeds expectations.'"
- "My evaluations were really good. They were stellar."
- "They were all just about perfect evaluations."
- "I always got the highest or second-highest possible score."
- "I had fifteen consecutive stellar evaluations. I was nationally prominent in my discipline."
- "My reviews were all stellar, and I even received merit bonuses."

Gail recalls having stellar evaluations too, with significant promotions and increased responsibilities.

Lori mentioned that her current boss hadn't ever done a performance review. It had been two years. "All the ones before her were excellent. How do I go from outstanding to terminated?"

These interviewees and others reported never having a bad review. From their perspective, the boss and the company were happy with their work. They felt confident that they were doing a good job and meeting the company's expectations. And they had written confirmation of that in their performance review.

The second group of people had a pattern of positive performance reviews until their new supervisor evaluated them. They then received reviews that were not like the others. A warning shot was fired.

Bruce described his last performance review, which "was the first negative evaluation I ever had. I felt the handwriting was on the wall. I'm not used to having a bad review." Bruce knew this change wasn't good, and he correctly anticipated that his job would be in jeopardy. He was fired two months later.

Similarly, Diane said, "Up until then, all excellent evaluations." Diane had been in the same company for twenty-eight years. Not only did Diane have significant tenure with the organization where she was promoted several times, she had written confirmation that she was a valued employee.

Elizabeth explained the situation in her new position: "Prior to my transferring to a new department, my evaluations were really good. I started reporting to a new supervisor. It was hard to get my arms around the way he did things. My boss's old boss was fired. The one before him left for a new job."

Although it wasn't bad, Randy was not comfortable with his last performance review. "I smelled something in my review, and when I gave the paper to my boss, she said, 'Do you think this is a performance improvement plan?' I said, 'It walks like a duck and talks like a duck.' She said it wasn't a performance plan, but the comment was directed by the CEO." Like Bruce, Randy sensed a difference in his performance review, but unlike Bruce, he directly confronted his supervisor. Randy didn't wait to be fired and orchestrated his own departure.

Some of the respondents didn't recognize the seriousness of their new supervisors' negative evaluation. They felt comfortable with their own performances. Elizabeth, Diane, and Wes did not understand the significance of their reviews and just accepted them as a new person's opinion. Others noticed that something was different. After years of positive performance reviews, they were now experiencing one that wasn't positive. Randy and Bruce recognized that the performance reviews indicated their jobs were in jeopardy.

The takeaway here is that a less-than-positive performance review—even if it's your only one—is a definite indicator of job vulnerability.

But as already pointed out, the opposite is not true: great performance evaluations do not necessarily mean job security. Wes commented, "I see it all the time where I work now. People get good reviews, and two months later they get terminated for a reason. If someone can make a better way (to do performance reviews), they should."

A few things are at work here. First, giving an employee realistic feedback is uncomfortable. Many managers would prefer not to engage in a difficult conversation. Consequently, sometimes people get satisfactory reviews even when they don't deserve them. Second, there are a lot of factors at play besides job performance that impact a person's job security, such as leadership transitions, economic considerations, and office politics and relationships. Third, an uncharacteristic poor or less-than-stellar performance review, *damning with faint praise*, should be taken as a serious warning that your job is in jeopardy.

## Praise

It may seem counterintuitive, but firings are often preceded by flattery. A couple of noteworthy ones come to mind. Ohio State University was under investigation for certain off-the-field activities of some of their football players. When asked in March 2011 whether the school had considered firing OSU head football coach Jim Tressel, a grinning President Gordon Gee said: "No, are you kidding? Let me just be very clear. I'm just hopeful the coach doesn't dismiss *me*." Coach Tressel resigned from his position two months later. Even though the university president's remark made it sound like Tressel was in the driver's seat, Tressel could not save his own job.

President George W. Bush famously and publicly praised FEMA (Federal Emergency Management Agency) director Michael Brown for his leadership in the recovery efforts just after Hurricane Katrina. His now famous line was, "You're doing a heck of a job, Brownie." The FEMA director resigned ten days later amid the controversy of how Katrina relief was handled.

After a few weeks on the job, Alexa received praise from her supervisor, "It shows so much of your character that you not only listen to my advice, but you implement it." "She was praising me. This is the opposite of what she said when she fired me!" During her termination meeting only a month later, Alexa's supervisor told her she didn't receive feedback well.

Karen was praised as well: "I was invited to a high-level meeting, where I had to give a report and have a conversation about quality-control and lean management processes in the firm. Afterward my boss e-mailed me, 'By the way, you were great at the leadership meeting.' Then he invited me to a cocktail party the group was having. Less than a month later, I was let go."

Gail recalled that her boss had told her she had led the "most important thing the organization had ever done." Despite his acknowledgment of her contribution, she was let go.

The flattery may be sincere, but it should not be taken as an indication your job is safe.

## Strong Performance

> "I built a new reporting structure and implemented
> a $12 million annualized margin improvement."
> —ANDREW

So the conventional wisdom is that people are fired because they aren't accomplishing their goals or doing their jobs well. But doing a great job isn't enough to keep a job. In fact, these interviewees recounted that they were fired after achieving a significant accomplishment.

Given a company's need to produce and succeed, I asked the interviewees what their accomplishments were prior to being let go. Were they really deadwood that needed to be let go, or did they make a difference in the company's performance and viability?

Here is a sampling of their responses:

Several interviewees like John believed that their bosses were threatened by them. John was in his late twenties at the beginning of his career. "I had just given a great presentation to the board of directors. Everyone liked it. I thought I was doing a great job. Right after the meeting, I was asked to come to my boss's office and he fired me. 'What! I just did this great thing, and now you're firing me?' He fired me. I was too good."

"I built a new reporting structure and implemented a $12 million annualized margin improvement," Andrew recalled. Saving a company $12 million is generally considered a huge accomplishment, but it was not enough to spare Andrew from losing his job.

Brenda recalled a big accomplishment just before she was fired. "I had just completed the organization's first successful fundraising event. We raised $100,000. I was the first executive in the history of the organization to develop and execute a successful fund-raising event. It was incredible—a big hit with the community. The board chair asked to meet with me. I walked in the room and saw him with our lawyer. They both looked serious. I knew they were going to fire me. So I said, 'I guess we're here to discuss how I leave.'"

Nick gathered his team to let them know their leader was let go and an interim leader would be named. He recalled their overconfidence: "They can't touch us, we're the rainmakers!" The new leader let everyone go and brought in his own team.

Exacerbated, Melissa shared, "I was thinking, 'They can't just let me go. We were very profitable. It was so shocking. How can you let someone go who's bringing in all this money, when you have a machine throughout the region? We were making money.'"

Kate related her major accomplishment: "I had just returned from the office with the news that I had landed a $3 million account. I was the person who had developed and nurtured the account and finally closed it. The account was one I had worked on for a long time. The client knew me, and I was to be their account manager. I returned from the client's and was told I was no longer needed. I was told to clean my things out. I asked, 'Who's going to service the account? They came because of me. They trusted me; that's why they signed.' I was told to clean my things out."

Given these accomplishments, it's easy to understand how people felt comfortable and confident in their positions. After all, most companies would covet record sales, perfect inspections, or a $12 million bottom-line improvement. Even though these significant accomplishments are not protections from being fired, they are yours, and you can use them to build your résumé. You will read later how important it is for you to track and record your accomplishments for future job hunting.

## Awarded

It's incredible that someone would be let go after just being recognized with an award. But that's what happened to four of the people interviewed.

In his first year with the company, Don was recognized with his company's internal award for engineering. While he was cleaning out his things after getting fired, his boss asked, "Don't you want this Innovation Award?" Don told him, "No, it would only bring bad memories of this day," and put it the garbage.

Renee was flown overseas for a week to receive a key award at her company's international recognition event. At the banquet she sat at the same table as the company's president. It was a huge honor for her. Naturally she was later shocked to hear that her position had been advertised and that her new boss was not committed to keeping her.

Recognized by his company one evening, Nick described the event and what happened in the days after. "We had our best year ever and celebrated with a dinner and recognition event. I was given a sculpture made by a local artist. When you were given one of these, you knew it was important. The leaders were praising my accomplishments. It was all such a convivial evening. I was proud of what I had done and very proud to receive the award. Everything felt like it was all going to work.

"We had a meeting a few days later with the new interim leader, and he started putting down my department, saying we had a terrible year. I was there in the room. And I was thinking, 'Didn't you just give me an award and public recognition?'" The next morning Nick returned the award to his new boss. He called a colleague at another institution to network. The colleague worked closely with Nick's boss and their department. He learned in this phone call that his interim leader was planning to let him go. Nick quickly escalated his job search and landed a new position.

Michelle worked her way up to a senior position in a consulting firm. She had recently been promoted and given a nice raise. In addition, she had received a company award and other honors and was asked to chair its internal council on minority issues. Although reluctant, at her friend's urging, Michelle went to an interview for another position while visiting family out of state. She was offered the job.

She had no plans to accept the position since she was very happy with her life and her job. When she returned from her trip back to work, she was fired. The termination was completely unexpected given all the honors Michelle had been given. Fortunately, she had explored the other position and was able to accept the job offer soon after.

Receiving an award in recognition of an accomplishment is an honor and a thrill, but it isn't a safeguard against getting fired. On the plus side, it does look good on a résumé and is a testament to excellent work.

## Promised a Promotion

> "I was heavily recruited by our company's largest competitor. I had a great job at an organization I loved. I wasn't looking to leave, but they kept calling. To get me they promised me a VP position in their corporate office."
> —MARK

Surprisingly, several of the people in this study were let go even after they were promised or offered a promotion. For most people, a pending promotion is a strong sign that the company and its leaders are invested in you. Once again the respondents felt especially confident about their future with their companies after being told they would be promoted.

Paula left her position at a large national retailer to take a new job with a promising future. "When I was hired, the head of my department said I would be his eventual successor. That was the main reason I took the job. It was a large, national, well-respected company. When my boss announced his retirement, he called me in to tell me I wouldn't be replacing him. He said that his boss didn't feel comfortable working with me. It was a big disappointment, but at least I could continue in my job.

"What I didn't know at the time was that one of my colleagues got a new job and turned in his resignation. They wanted to keep him, so they promised him his boss's job. Then they needed a spot for his former boss whose job he was getting. They didn't want to fire him, so they gave him part of my job.

"After my original boss retired, the CEO hired Ben for the position I was originally promised. Ben became my boss. Then he got a new boss. He and his boss traveled all over the country meeting with associates. When they finished their national tour of the stores together, Ben was fired. He had traveled for months on behalf of the company, away from his wife and kids. He asked the CEO why he was being fired. The CEO simply said, 'No reason, employment at will.' Later he learned he was replaced by a person who had worked in a similar position for the CEO at his old company.

Paula advises, "It's not about how good a job you do; it's about who wants to work with you. It's all about managing up." Managing up means to use various methods to make your manager's job easier and to make yourself a valuable asset to your company. It can also mean making an intentional effort to manage the one who is supposed to manage you.

Mark shared how he was similarly promised a promotion. "I was heavily recruited by our company's largest competitor. I had a great job at an organization I loved. I wasn't looking to leave, but they kept calling. To get me they promised me a VP position in their corporate office doing organizational development—OD is my passion. They told me I would start out as head of one of their locations, and after a year or two, would move to the VP role full time. That would have been my dream job, but after six months they fired me. They didn't give me enough time."

Mark continued with advice for others: "If you are promised a position of acceleration after a year, that should scare you. 'You'll come in at this level, and in a year you'll be at this level.' Alarm bells should go off. It's a compromise that they aren't prepared to do. I was incredibly intuitive before I moved. I was thorough. I made them write up their promise to me in the offer letter. They are using the assets they have to get you and promising you the moon to get you. I was lied to."

Helen worked as a fund-raiser at a prestigious private school. She advanced to become a senior director. Her boss, the head of the fund-raising department, was planning his retirement and tapped Helen to be his successor. She had accepted the position. One of the major donors to the school asked Helen's boss to set up a time for him to meet Helen. Following the meeting, the donor called up Helen's boss and told him he didn't think Helen was experienced enough to assume the leadership role. The offer of a promotion was rescinded. After that, Helen, deflated was unable to stay in her position.

Don also believed he would be promoted. "During the interview process, my future manager had a closed-door meeting with me where he confided that he was on the fast track and slated to move up the ladder with the department manager and that I was to be groomed as his replacement." Don was fired eighteen months later.

A department head, Frank was tapped to take over the entire department. He patiently waited for his promotion, supporting the current department head. Before he could assume his new position, the position he was promised, he was fired. The boss brought in his best friend instead. Frank had to relocate his family a few months later when he landed a new job.

In this research there were more stories of people promised a promotion only to be let go later. Promises of promotion are not binding, things change. Moreover, the promise of a promotion does not even mean job security. The lesson is that despite the promise of further advancement in the company, you are not fireproof.

# Promoted

> "The thing is—I had just been promoted to
> a specialized sales and service team."
> —LEE

Ann Curry, a reporter and on-air personality at NBC, was promoted to co-anchor of the *Today* show. She was fired after her first year there. She famously said goodbye on the air: "For all of you who saw me as a ground-breaker, I'm sorry I couldn't carry the ball to the finish line, but, man, I did try," Ms. Curry said with a choked voice. "And so to all of you who watch, thank you from the bottom of my heart for letting me touch yours."

Ms. Curry made a point of reminding her employer of all the feats she had accomplished on the network's behalf, though she addressed the viewers. "*You* are the real *Today* show family," Ms. Curry said into the camera. "You are why I have ventured into dangerous places and interviewed dictators and jumped out of planes and off of bridges and climbed mountains and landed in the South Pole and convinced the Dalai Lama to come live in our studio."

Like Ann Curry, several of the interviewees were promoted shortly before being let go.

- Diane said she got along well with her new boss. "At first things were going well. He liked me, I liked him. He promoted me to director." Diane was fired a few months later.
- Melissa shared that she had a big promotion after working five years at her company. "I was promoted to a VP less than a year before I was fired."
- Lee had been with his company for six years when he was fired. "I had just been promoted to a specialized sales and service team. Had I stayed in my old job as a technician, I probably would have still had a job."
- Julie spoke of her promotion: "Our HR department had switched me from hourly to salaried within three months of getting laid off."

## Asked Not to Quit

> "He begged me, 'I don't want you to quit.'"
> —ELIZABETH

Perhaps the most extreme example of false assurances comes from Elizabeth. She had admittedly not jelled well with her new boss. "It was weird the last couple of months. I only had this boss for a year. Three bosses in two years.

"I wrote up my letter of resignation, and I gave it to my boss's boss, the division head. He gave it back to me. 'I need you to stay.' He begged me, 'I don't want you to quit.' I said, 'I can't take my new boss. I cannot take this.' He said, 'Just take a day and think about it. He gave the letter back and said, 'You keep it.'"

Elizabeth stayed in her position until one day she received an e-mail from her boss's boss with a meeting request at four o'clock. "When I walked into the division head's office, the HR person was sitting there. I was thinking to myself, 'This is not good.' And the division leader began to tell me that he 'didn't think I was happy there anymore.' He felt it was best that we separate."

A similar dynamic happened to Gail. She recalled, "My boss begged me to stay with the company. He gave me a significant raise to stay. He fought hard to have me stay. Salary and bonus. He said, 'You can do whatever you want, just don't leave.' Things were good. There was a year-long honeymoon. We worked side by side. He relied on me and allowed me to do good things. I had free reign." As said earlier, after taking a maternity leave, Gail was fired.

For most people, being asked not to quit would be a strong signal of support from their employer. It would be perfectly normal to assume job security. However, even those who are begged not to quit were not fireproof.

# Promised Job Security

> "No one is going to lose their job."
> — CAROL'S DIVISION LEADER

Presidential candidate George McGovern, in defending his running mate, Thomas Eagleton, famously said, "I am behind him one thousand percent." Eighteen days later Eagleton withdrew from the ticket at McGovern's request. A *Time* magazine poll taken at the time found that 77 percent of the respondents said Eagleton's medical record would not affect their vote. Nonetheless, the press made frequent references to his "shock therapy," and McGovern feared this would detract from his campaign platform.

It may happen that an employee begins to sense the landscape is changing at his or her company. Perhaps the company has taken some losses or had some bad publicity. Or maybe there has been a change in leadership. It's natural and perhaps wise for employees to wonder if their jobs are safe. Several of our interviewees experienced this insecurity. They recalled how they were told their job was safe.

Karen described how her boss calmed the anxiety of his leadership team once it was announced the company was sold. "Before meeting the company's new owner, the boss brought the team together. He wanted to assure the team that although there was a new owner, we would be safe. 'Everyone here has made it. You are all in. Relax. You don't have to try to impress anyone. You are the team,' the boss claimed. But three weeks later, a colleague was let go. I was out nine months later. Several more followed."

"I was aware that things were changing," Julie acknowledged. "We weren't making money in my program. I was up-front. I asked if there were changes pending. I was reassured nothing was changing. I was assured I had job security. I was encouraged to go to grad school, so I did. My supervisor had assured me that I would never lose my job after I had been prepped. I had been given opportunities to provide leadership to different things. I was being groomed to become something better. Three months later I was let go."

During a difficult economy, Carol was assured her job was safe. The recession was affecting her company's business. Her division leader told his team they would have to reduce their costs. They were willing to do that, but everyone was anxious about their job security. To reassure his team, he said, "No one is going to lose their job." Carol exhaled a big sigh of relief. But two weeks later the division leader and her boss met with her. "They told me my job would be eliminated. I had three months. But he had said no one would lose their job!"

This is an important finding of this research: *even if you are told your job is safe, it may not be.* You may be thinking of buying a house, having a child, or taking an expensive vacation. Before you take the next step, you want to get a handle on how stable your job is. Your evaluations are solid. You have had some noteworthy accomplishments. Your boss tells you she knows of no pending changes in the company. Or he tells you that you are doing a great job, and he wants to keep you. Your job may be safe, or it may be in jeopardy. Either way, understand that the affirmation or assurances of a boss is not a guarantee that your job will be safe.

What's the lesson here? Job insecurity is the new normal. Employment at will is the law in most states for salaried employees, those who are exempt from overtime pay. That means the employer does not need a reason to fire someone. It also means that doing a good job, being loyal, and working hard are sometimes not enough to keep one's job.

The purpose of this book is not to make you fearful, but to make you aware. Most of my interviewees reported strong work performance, positive evaluations, praise, and sometimes even promotions and awards. Their excellence was not enough to provide them with job security. Awareness of workplace realities will enable you to be better prepared for any contingencies described in this book.

## Key Takeaways:

1. Employment at will is the law in most states for exempt, salaried employees. You can be fired for any reason.

2. Be sure you record and keep copies of your performance reviews, awards, and other evidence of your outstanding work. These are vital to have when you craft your résumé and interview for new positions.

3. Do not take positive recognition, promotions, awards, or assurances of job security as an indicator you are fireproof. You aren't.

# CHAPTER 4

## FIRE ESCAPE: TAKING ACTION WHEN YOU SEE THE SIGNS

> "Exit visas are imminent."
> —GORDON GECKO, IN THE FILM *WALL STREET*, 1987

I n chapter 3, I shared some of the signs that, as the famous line from the movie *Wall Street* goes, "Exit visas are imminent." While the signs often weren't evident in real time, in hindsight the interviewees shared the signs that their jobs were in jeopardy. As such, firings came as a total shock for the majority of my interviewees.

Several of them, though, heeded the warning shots that their jobs were at risk. They recognized that it wasn't working, took the lead on creating an exit plan, and resigned to avoid being fired.

In his late twenties, Jeff had an emerging career in the business world. However, work was becoming more and more stressful. He felt beat down and unappreciated by his boss and upper management, and it was jarring his confidence. He realized his job was in jeopardy. "I saw the signs. I was accepted for graduate school on Tuesday, and I resigned on Friday." Fortunately, Jeff had saved some money to get him by short term. And if all else failed, Jeff said, "I have a supportive family." Although he felt put down by his employer, he rationalized, "I figure that an Ivy League university and my company can't both be right."

Randy described how he identified that his job was in jeopardy: "It probably started last summer. I had not had a good feeling or good relations with the CEO. He was there beyond his time. He should have retired. I am not a person that wants to sit around. I thought my boss would be the next CEO. I know the CEO got involved in my last review. The review said I 'need to work on relationships with senior leaders.' I could see his handiwork was in there.

"Pretty soon I was thinking, 'Hey, I'm the idiot here. You hired me to change, so let me do that.' That's when I started thinking, 'This isn't going right.' They didn't want to change, that's all. And I did. They wanted to keep things as they were. I think paying *anyone* to do nothing is stupid. I went to them and said, 'Listen, why don't we just not renew my contract?' At first they said no, they wanted me to stay.

"That was when I said, 'I'm out.' I had to get out under my own direction and my own thinking.

"I went to my boss, who I had been mentoring; she was interviewing at other companies too. We talked about the budget and goals. I told her 'You don't need me. Why don't you wait till a new CEO comes in and hire a high-level person at that time?'

"She told the CEO, and the CEO said, 'Make it happen.' A month later I got the contract and then gave them a plan for how to continue without me. I did more than I should have. I should have said, 'Fix it yourself.' Once I said, 'Let's make the change,' it moved quickly. I offered to continue working for six months while looking for another job. My boss said no. I was out."

After serving with a large health institution for four years, Paula initiated discussions for her own departure: "My boss was crazy, really unstable. She had big mental health problems. One day she was happy and upbeat, the next she was down and miserable. She didn't have a family; work was all she had. She kept criticizing my performance. She wanted things done that were not realistic, not in our world. She wanted to say all the requisitions she had received were completed. That just doesn't happen in our business. She wanted to put me on a performance improvement plan. When I realized I couldn't be successful working for her, I went to her boss, Ken.

"Ken was aware of her mood swings and her craziness but didn't want to confront it. His job was changing; he was transitioning to a new job at the corporate office. He wasn't going to stick his neck out on his way out the door. I couldn't take it. So rather than endure her constant criticism and mood swings, I asked Ken if he would support severancing me out. He agreed. I left the company with some severance and vacation pay. So I ended up having the summer off and spent time at the pool with friends while I looked for a job."

Like Paula and Randy, Renee saw the writing on the wall. "My boss left the company, and I considered returning to my former position. It was open, and I could have gone back to it. I was worried about how things would go with a new boss. Then her boss called me and asked me not to go back to my old job, but to stay in my current role. She gave me the impression that she was looking out for me, that she wanted me in this department." But when the new boss took over, she told Renee that staying at her job wasn't guaranteed, that she would have to reapply for her position and compete with others to get the job.

"It made me sick. I didn't know what to do. I talked to my parents and my husband. Every day I wondered if it would be the last day. I checked to see if I could get my old job back, the one that was open to me earlier and my boss's boss talked me out of taking. Someone else took that job. I couldn't go there. I was sick. I didn't know what to do, but then again, I didn't really have a choice.

"Then I got lucky. A guy in the company heard what was happening to me. We went to the same college. He ran a totally different department. He thought what happened to me stank and said he had a job for me. I interviewed with him and got the job. It was the same salary, but I would no longer be eligible for a bonus. I took the job. And I am learning everything from scratch. I am excited, but I don't know what I'm doing yet. Both of the other people whose jobs were posted are gone. One left on his own; one was not rehired.

"It's true; I may have been rehired for my old job. She could have picked me after her search. But why search if you are happy with your team? I couldn't take the risk. I learned my lesson. Now I know."

A twenty-two-year-old college student, Kristin, shared how she faced a difficult situation: "So I heard about the job through a friend. The job was a front-desk person who also does a little cleaning and administrative work at an athletic club, a small gym run by an inexperienced manager.

"She hired me after five minutes: 'OK, you have the job.' She scheduled me for training three times. I came in two times; the third time I had a class seminar so I had to miss it. That's as far as I got.

"The training wasn't paid—*that* wasn't told to me beforehand. I never set foot in an orientation. I asked the girl who got me the job how to let people know you need a day off. She told me to tell the shift supervisor I was scheduled with and it would be fine. So I told the guy who was working at the time. He said to come in next time. That ended up not being the proper way to handle it.

"The boss communicated through texts—passive aggressive, with twenty back-and-forth texts, all about why I handled it so poorly. I wasn't told how to handle it. I didn't have the rules. I can't follow them if I don't know them.

"My boss's problem with me was that I didn't e-mail her. My friend told me to tell the shift supervisor. I did. But she was still upset with me. I said, 'OK, I won't do it again.' I apologized. 'Sorry for the communication error.' This is all texting.

"She texted back: 'Do not come back to work until we have a conversation about what you've done.' I texted, 'OK, I won't.'

"She told my friend she would call me in the morning. She didn't tell me that. I wasn't prepared. I got the call. She said, 'We need to have a talk about protocol.' I said, 'I think that would be a good idea. I haven't had an orientation. I haven't even filled out my tax form, because no one gave them to me.

"She was like, 'We need to go over this stuff.' The only protocol she went over with me was that I have to call her if I can't make a shift. And that was it. No other rules. She just wanted to say it again to me on the phone. She said, 'Do you have other questions?'

"I said, 'Yeah, I want to know the other rules. Do you have a packet or something?' And she got irritated with me. I said, 'I feel like we're not communicating well. I am not receptive to text messages to communicate about business. And the fact that you are talking to other employees about me isn't helpful to my success.' She talked to more than one of my friends about me.

"And then she said something, but it wasn't nice. I can't remember what she said. I said, 'I think the way that we approach business communication is very different. It won't be mutually beneficial to us. So I think me working here won't be beneficial to us. My next shift will be my last. Thank you for the opportunity.

"I one hundred percent thought she would fire me. I got off the train." Although she barely started work, Kristin could tell the situation was not going to work out.

"After putting together, a successful event," Brenda started, "the board chair asked to meet with me. I walked in the room and saw him with our lawyer. They both looked serious. I had been through this two times before. This third time I preempted because I knew I was about ready to be fired. So I said, 'I guess we're here to discuss how I leave.'

"Since I knew they were going to fire me, I looked at the board chair and said, 'I don't think this is working out. I'm not what you want. It's best if I resign. I am happy to give you notice, whatever you want.' He said, 'OK, you can leave now.' I said, 'OK.' 'I will give you a couple hours to pick up your belongings.' 'It won't take me long to pick up a coffee cup.' I never brought anything personal to that office. I knew from day one it was short term.

"Here's the best part of the story. I had three firings in a row. But here's the good part. I came home, and my husband said, 'Oh my gosh, you quit your job.' I said, 'How did you know?' He said, 'You're smiling.' I look back now and know that if I had not been fired, I would not have gotten this great job—my dream job. And I've been here ten years."

After being let go previously, Nick watched his new work environment carefully. He relocated his family and rented a home. After a year he asked his boss how stable things looked and whether Nick should now be looking at buying a house and settling in. "My boss recommended renting. He was later demoted, and I saw the writing on the wall this time. I started my job search." The interim leader who replaced Nick's boss let the whole team go. Fortunately, Nick's job search had landed him a couple of offers, and he was able to resign before receiving notice that he was terminated.

Lee experienced conflicts with his boss at an entertainment company. His boss wanted margins that Lee didn't think were feasible in a smaller market. "We couldn't get those kinds of markups here. Sales were down. So instead of that being the problem, I became the problem." He too saw the writing on the wall. He began to make plans to start his own business. "Then I overheard my coworkers colluding on how they were going to divide up my leads when I was gone. That was confirmation that he was going to fire me."

Lee's boss eventually called a meeting with him. Lee knew what was coming and prepared a letter of resignation. "If you aren't in the loop or aren't part of the future, you are on your way out. I gave him the letter of resignation and my notice before he could fire me." Lee started his own business.

Like the others, Janice anticipated that she was going to lose her job the way her colleague had. Two of Janice's coworkers told her that they heard she would be leaving. "I thought, 'They are getting ready to fire me.' So I got done at the office and left to go to one of our branches, convinced that they were going to fire me. Somewhere on my way to the branch, I called a friend and asked her to write me a resignation letter. My boss and human resources had planned a meeting with me. I wanted it in my hand in case they were going to fire me. I needed to resign instead of being fired because I needed insurance and my vacation pay.

"Another person who worked there got no vacation pay, so I was worried that would happen to me. After my coworker was fired, I knew I had to get my stuff organized and my files in order so I could hand them off to someone and take my personal stuff off the computer. It was difficult to do. I got an external hard drive and could work off that instead of the virtual private network, which had connection problems. I moved my files. I didn't delete anything work related. I only put back things people after me would need. I didn't take any work files.

"That triggered the IT department to report it to HR. So then I talked to four of them at a meeting where they accused me of taking files and deleting them. I told them everything was on a hard drive. 'You need to put it back.' That's when the IT person took my files and gave them to three of my colleagues. They never told me they did it. I had a friend in IT who confirmed it.

"They were treating me like a thief, like I was stealing files that I shouldn't have when I was really trying to organize things for whoever they hired after me. 'You know that's against the policy to have a flash drive.' I wasn't trying to keep anything from them. I was simply trying to get it organized. Afterward I went back to work and thought they were going to call me in to the office and say I stole things and violated the policy.

"So they called another meeting. I walked in, and before the HR person could say anything, I gave her my notice." Janice didn't have another job lined up but did get paid for her accrued vacation days. She found work immediately as a subcontractor in her field and got a full-time position a few months later.

Lesley had a chilling experience that caused her to leave before she was laid off. "I was in charge of a new building. We were doing well. Our renovation was complete, we were ahead of budget, and we opened ahead of schedule. It was exciting to be doing so well. After a meeting, a corporate human resources person asked to see me in my office. She told me that I was performing well, too well. She said I was making the rest of the team look bad. She wasn't complimenting me; she was angry.

"I was shaken, shocked. I knew after that I was a marked woman. She was going to get me fired. I talked to my boss, and he said I should figure out how to get along with her. I knew right then I had to leave."

But Lesley didn't leave right away. "I knew I had to keep my hand in many projects. I never said no to anything for one reason: I was making myself indispensable. I knew the projects would help me gain the experience needed to launch my consulting business. I wanted to be able to write my ticket when I was ready to leave. I wanted to be sure that would be my leap into consulting."

Then the company began to show signs of financial strain. "I started to figure out that when it was time for cuts, I would be one of them. That made me decide the time was right."

Lesley anticipated that they would need her to stay on part time as a consultant when she left. "When I decided to leave, I wanted to jump-start my consulting business. My boss asked me to write down what I had been working on. A half hour later he said, 'I had no idea you were doing all this.' I got myself so entrenched, I was indispensable. I made them an offer to continue to work as a consultant. I had two big projects I could take with me for eighteen months as a project manager. That was my way of getting back at them. They couldn't say no—I was involved in so many projects that I made myself indispensable."

The stories included in this chapter depict people who took matters into their own hands. They suspected they were going to be let go, and they implemented their own exit strategies. Approaching an employer about working out your departure may be a welcome relief for them. It takes the heat off their having to fire you and create unpleasantness in the workplace. Be sure to be ready to leave at once if you do. While it may be your wish to work out a transition, the employer may not want you around. Randy offered to stay on and help with the transition of his replacement but was told to leave immediately. And Sam told his new boss he knew things weren't working out and would start to look for a new job. His boss fired him soon after. Be ready to leave if you suggest the idea of a planned transition.

## Key Takeaways

1. When the signs appear, pay attention to them and take them seriously.
2. When things don't seem to be working out, consider taking matters into your own hands and planning for a possible departure.
3. If you suspect you will be terminated, you may wish to consult an attorney.
4. Always have a plan B. Be ready for anything to happen. (See chapter 11.)
5. Do not offer your company an exit strategy unless you are prepared to leave immediately.

# CHAPTER 5

## BURN NOTICE: BEING BLACKBALLED BY YOUR FORMER EMPLOYER

> "Good God, I must have leprosy."
> —NICK

The TV show *Burn Notice* made the words in its title popular. Lasting seven seasons on the USA Network, *Burn Notice* was about a spy who was not just fired, he was "burned." Intelligence agencies issue burn notices to discredit agents or sources or to announce their firing when they become unreliable or ineffective. A burn notice means that the person is excommunicated from the intelligence agency.

While the phrase *burn notice* isn't typically used in business, the activity exists nonetheless. In this context, burn notice refers to employers who have closed out employment opportunities in their own companies for someone they have let go or those who have signaled to other companies in their field that someone is unhirable. In effect, the employee is blackballed. The impact of losing a job is compounded when it's accompanied by burn notice.

When someone separates from a company, regardless of what the company calls it—a termination, layoff, reduction in force, or separation—the company will typically decide if the person is eligible for rehire or not eligible for rehire. One might expect that those who were fired would not be eligible for being rehired at that company. Likewise, one would assume that a company would not declare someone ineligible for rehire if he or she was laid off or if his or her position was eliminated.

The concept of a burn notice is well illustrated by the following stories of six people who experienced one.

With fifteen years at a large organization, Nick expected to readily find work elsewhere in the company when his position was eliminated. He looked everywhere. "I called a key leader in our system and asked if he could use me somewhere else in the organization. After all, I had a strong track record while I was in that department. He told me he couldn't think of any opportunities that were open, but suggested volunteering in one of them for a while. Another department head suggested I take an entry-level position in my field and grovel and act like I was really grateful for it.

"I went to two other managers who had open positions I was qualified for. I went in person and met with each one. I said, 'Oh, I see you have a position open.' They would nod to say yes, they did. Then I would say I was interested in applying for that position. They would avoid eye contact and say they didn't think so. Little did I know I was on the do-not–resuscitate list.

"I called everyone I knew at the institution, including the guy who was a recruiter in my former division, because I saw that my old job became available. I had set the standard that all people following me had not met. As I talked to people I realized, people aren't really listening to me when I tell them about my desire to stay at the organization. They're taking my meeting, but they're not going to hire me. They've already made up their minds.

"I pursued every avenue and realized there was something preventing me from continuing here. People I worked with for twelve to fifteen years basically stopped talking to me. People couldn't make eye contact. Good God, I must have leprosy.

"My last meeting was with the new head of our department. I said, 'John, I have had a great time here, and I would like to continue in another capacity. I want to ask for your support. I am going to find my next great opportunity.' Sitting in a massive office at one end of a small table, I asked for his support. He wasn't helping. He murmured some small talk like, 'I wish you the best.' I had let him know I had been loyal to the organization, and I could tell he wasn't going to offer help. I directly asked him, 'Can I count on your support during my search?' He got up from the table, walked across the long office, and sat at his desk. No eye contact. His final words were 'Marilyn will show you out.'"

Despite his fifteen years in the organization, and even though his position was eliminated, Nick was issued a burn notice. As he experienced, it was as if everyone in the organization got the word *not* to help him. Nick's accomplishments weren't enough to get him back in a position at the institution, except for the audacity of one person who suggested he volunteer in the organization for a while. He fell out of favor because people perceived him as being aligned with his former boss, who was fired. He wasn't given the opportunity to demonstrate that he could be a loyal team player under a new regime. Nick aptly referred to it as being on the DNR—do not resuscitate—list.

Likewise, Paula shared her experience of being burn listed. She had great difficulty working for her immediate supervisor, who Paula claimed had unrealistic expectations. Rather than waiting to be fired, Paula took the lead in planning her own separation. She worked out a deal with her boss's boss to be severanced out of her job. After Paula had left, a new division vice president was recruited for her old department. It did not take her long to fire Paula's former boss. Paula shared, "I was so happy when I heard that. I reached out to her to see if she would be open to talking to me. I really liked the company and wanted to see if I could return. I sent her an e-mail congratulating her and offering to have coffee if she would like to meet. She responded very positively. At first I thought she was open to my returning, but she ended up bringing in someone who worked with her at her last employer. Unfortunately, my exit agreement included a clause stating I was ineligible to work at the company again."

Paula experienced a typical burn notice. Many severance agreements prohibit the employee from being rehired to work anywhere within the organization after being let go and signal future managers of this fact. In Paula's case the organization validated her concern by firing her former boss. Even after acknowledging the problem with Paula's former supervisor, the organization would not consider her for a position.

Susan worked as a location manager for one of the largest and most successful national chains. Her branch was growing rapidly, and the organization was thriving. Then, Susan became ill and had to take a leave of absence. Her corporate office needed to fill her position to keep the organization moving forward. When she recovered, she asked to be reassigned to another branch. Her children were in school, so she only asked to be placed somewhere in the greater metropolitan area. Susan's corporate office would not accommodate her request. They offered her only small locations in small towns, hours away from home, even though several locations had openings in her area.

In Susan's case the headquarters' unwillingness to place her in her local market was tantamount to her losing her job. She returned from sick leave to learn that the only way she could return to work was to move to a rural location. Susan left the organization and was out of work for more than six months before landing a new position.

Recall that after seven years as a frontline manager, Julie's position was eliminated. "They wanted to eliminate my position six months earlier, but the boss was too busy to do it. I was lucky. I asked if there were other open positions. They were not willing to look for me. I wasn't being fired; I was being laid off. That's what they told me. Why won't you look for a new position for me? I looked at HR and I lost it. I felt very betrayed." Even though there were no stated performance concerns, the organization would not allow her to seek other employment there. She was given a burn notice.

Don talked about how the stigma of being fired from one position has followed him: "I have noticed after being let go from my job that companies often will become excited about me and approach strongly. In some cases, they seemed so eager to hire me, but then just as immediately went cold. In my two most recent positions, sometime within two months of my being hired, they found out I was dismissed. In both cases I had proven myself by that time, but it is forever a black spot on my career."

After more than twenty years of service, Mona was fired from her organization. "That was bad enough. Then a position came up that I thought I would be a good candidate for. It was local, and many people in the organization encouraged me to apply. However, the organization that fired me got word to them that it would be awkward if I worked there. They did business together. So they didn't hire me. I was blackballed."

After losing her job at a hospital, Lori sued her former employer. "After being fired I saw an attorney who thought we had a valid case. We took depositions and in fact found out that my boss had been lying and falsely accused me. She was deposed and admitted under oath that some of it was stretched and fabricated. A prior boss admitted under oath that I was exemplary. I didn't win the suit, but I felt vindicated that she had admitted she falsified the information she used to fire me. Then, she was fired. I did get the satisfaction of proving they lied. They could have brought me back, but because of the lawsuit, they didn't. The HR director would not allow me to be rehired." Even though the accusations against Lori were proven false, and the person who made them was fired, her hospital would not reinstate her. She was burn listed instead.

Connie, the attorney who was fired after twenty-eight years at her firm, offered this advice about suing an employer: "Just because you are over forty, female, or black—just because you can file a lawsuit, doesn't mean you should. There are not a lot of protections out there. I could have, but you get a reputation for suing. The community is small; they hear things. You need to move on.

"It takes a lot out of you to sue. The hurdle for punitive damages is high. There is a cap on discrimination claims. Employment claims are expensive and fact intensive: four hundred to six hundred exhibits. It's like a divorce. They are very emotional. I would see people taking their retirement out to fund a lawsuit. Had you sued, it would have been hard to find another job in your profession. If it's high profile, it's in the news-papers. With media now, it's easy to see who's suing. People won't hire you if they know you have sued a former employer."

Of course, every situation is different, but Connie cautions that an-other way to be burn listed by other companies is to be known as some-one who sues an employer.

Being burn listed adds insult to injury. Having to deal with the loss of a job and getting geared up for a new job search is difficult enough. Discovering that the organization will not help you after a layoff or job elimination is devastating. Finding out it has tarnished your repu-tation to others makes recovery and rebounding exponentially more challenging.

## Key Takeaways

1. Do your best to never burn a bridge.
2. Develop positive relationships outside of your organization. If you're given a burn notice, these relationships will help to minimize its negative effects.
3. Even if your company knows you were wronged, once you are let go, it is unlikely they will re-hire you.
4. To find a new job after a burn notice, you may need to relocate or change fields until the smoke clears.

# CHAPTER 6

## FIRE-EXIT STRATEGY: FORMULATING AN EXIT STRATEGY

> "Always have your exit story ready to go."
> — GAIL

*Job uncertainty is the new normal. Employment at will is a reality.* At any time and for any reason, you could lose your job, no matter how good or how loyal an employee you are, without being offered a rationale, reason, or explanation. It is routine today for companies to buy, sell, and merge with other companies. Transitions happen. Leaders change. And economic hard times can result in layoffs. When we don't have specific protections, jobs bring no guarantees. As Melissa aptly and succinctly advises, "Work every day like it's your last day."

Sometimes new hires sign an employment contract that will spell out many of the terms of a separation. This is similar to a prenuptial agreement. Though a separation agreement may be part of the initial employment process, it may also be offered in other instances. These agreements outline the terms of the discharge—including severance pay (if any), vacation pay, health care, and other items—in exchange for protecting the employer's reputation through a nondisparagement clause and the employer's confidential information. Sometimes it also includes a noncompete clause or nonsolicitation of other employees. Most important, the benefits usually are provided in exchange for the employee's agreement not to sue. They are often but not always used in terminating exempt employees.

It is important to get expert legal advice when negotiating employment or severance agreements. These and other legal aspects of an employment separation are not the focus of this chapter. Naturally, anyone in this position will be focused on such essential bread-and-butter issues. They are all critical, practical elements of dealing with a job loss, and there are plenty of qualified resources for you on these topics. Simply put, seek legal advice for legal questions.

This chapter is about how to position yourself in the best light possible, despite the circumstances. It will focus on nonlegal aspects of an exit strategy, including crafting an exit story. An exit story—the narrative you tell people about why you left your company—is vital. Frame your exit in such a way that you can enhance employability once you leave.

Those who have been fired recommend preparing an exit strategy *before you are let go*. When Gail was let go, she was presented the choice to stay on the job for a month or leave immediately. "I knew it would be hard to stay for a month—to be around them—but my loyalty to the team trumped the awkward and intense atmosphere. Then I proceeded to figure out my key messages. That would be a tip I would give anyone who thought they were going to be fired or were looking for a new job. You need an exit story."

The exit story might include answering the following questions:

- How will your employer communicate to your coworkers that you are leaving?
- What will they say to others, including employees and other companies, about why you left?
- Will you get a reference letter?
- How do you announce to others your newfound availability?
- How do you explain the gap on your résumé if you don't get a new job right away?
- What do you say in an interview about why you left your past employer?

Several of these aspects of a fire-exit strategy may be in your control. Being aware of them will help you at the time of job loss. This part of your exit strategy will help you manage your reputation. And in many cases, it will help your employer as well. I'll get to that later.

## Keep Your Composure

Human resource experts generally recommend that termination meetings be sure and swift. HR often has a checklist of things to do while talking to the employee. They are likely to start the meeting by saying the decision is final and nonnegotiable. During this meeting, however, or even during a follow-up call, you have the opportunity to build your exit strategy. The most important thing to do in this meeting is to keep your composure and remain professional and polite. You may be angry, scared, shocked, dismayed, devastated, upset, or all of these, but do not convey your emotions at this time. Keep your composure. It's better to remain silent than say something you will regret.

Ann Curry remained poised and polished during the meeting where she was let go. Her employer mistakenly thought she was coping well with the decision and had no idea she would use her on-air departure to share her sadness. By keeping her composure, Ann Curry was allowed to say goodbye on air and consequently say what she wanted to her viewers and her mentors.

"This is not how I expected to ever leave this couch after fifteen years," she admitted. "But I am so grateful, especially to all of you who watch. We often call ourselves a family, but you are the real *Today* show family. You are why I've ventured into dangerous places and interviewed dictators and jumped out of planes and climbed mountains...I have loved you, and I have wanted to give you the world, and I still do. I'm sorry I couldn't carry the ball over the finish line. But man, did I try."

## Immediate Response

The same is true when telling others about your departure. You will need to be selective as to who you share your true feelings with. For anyone outside your inner circle, stick to a script. Here is an excellent example of someone who did this:

This post was made on Facebook by a young mother who had just lost her job: "Tonight I packed up my office and left work for the last time. Eric felt it was time we part ways. I left with grace and class. I smiled; I cracked a few jokes and held my head high." People pressed her to find out what happened. She responded that she and her boss just "didn't click, nothing hostile, but we never found common ground." She ended by saying she loved the organization and hoped this was the right decision for all involved.

While I don't recommend posting your departure from a company on social media, I do think the tone and spirit of this exit story are positive. And, importantly, she shared her positive feelings for the company, avoided blaming, and didn't burn that bridge. This is a believable story. Moreover, people commented on her announcement, trying to get more information, but she wisely stuck to her original script.

One of the people interviewed for this book did just the opposite. Julie, another young mother, was let go after seven years at her company. With her emotions raw, she went home after being fired and posted an angry rant on Facebook. Many people commented, and through her responses she voiced even more anger, resentment, and bitterness. And she named her company. A former colleague of hers saw it and advised her to take the entire posting down, which she did. No employer wants to hear someone bad-mouth another employer. It demonstrates a lack of discretion and professionalism.

If your emotions are raw, if you are upset, fearful, or angry, do not talk to people about being let go, and do not put anything in writing on social media, in letters, or in an e-mail. It may feel good to vent, but it will do more damage to your reputation and your career. Try to take the high road, and if you can't, don't say anything. You can always express your feelings in a private journal to vent some of those emotions.

Julie's friends continued to bring up the topic and get her to talk about it, and as she realized, this commiserating wasn't letting her move on. She had to put those friendships aside.

So the first part of your exit strategy is to maintain your composure and professionalism.

## Working with Your Employer on the Exit Story

> "I asked him if we could agree to say that
> my departure was part of the organization's
> leadership transition. He agreed."
> —KAREN

If you have the opportunity, work with your employer on your exit story. Ask your employer if you can craft together the script for why you left. This is not difficult if you were laid off or if your position was eliminated. In these cases, the economic reality of the company required some position cuts. An employer will likely not say you were fired since that could be considered character defamation. So if you are able to influence how the company communicates your departure, ask if you can draft something yourself for their approval. Your exit e-mail to colleagues and clients should be positive and professional. "Talk about how great it was to work with them and wish them the best," says Louise Kursmark of Best Impression Career Services in Reading, Massachusetts.

The following example was sent from the employee's company e-mail, with the company's permission, to employees, vendors, and colleagues outside of the organization.

Dear Colleagues,

I wanted to let you know that I am leaving my position at _____.
It was an exciting opportunity to engineer a new quality assurance process, and I'm proud of the many accomplishments the team made. I wish you and the company continued success.

I'm pursuing other opportunities that have presented themselves to me over the past six months. As you know, this field is expanding rapidly, and this is an exciting time for new technologies, connections, and innovations.

Below is my updated contact information. I look forward to staying in touch!

This e-mail announces the employee's departure as if it were her idea. It also preserves goodwill between the organization, the employee, and the remaining employees. And let's face it, it is far better than the usual "Effective March 2, Joe Smith is no longer employed at ABC Company." In her book *Organizational Behavior: Real Research for Real Managers*, Dr. Jone Pearce encourages companies to allow departing employees to draft and send the announcement themselves, after the company has approved it. This demonstrates goodwill and sensitivity that will not be lost on remaining employees. She also advises managers to cite the employee's accomplishments and publicly thank him or her for his or her work.

It's helpful for all involved if the employer and employee come together to share the same story regarding a termination. Ashley was terminated from a senior position at a regional real estate firm. She explained, "A new leader was appointed. I just knew she wanted to pick her own team. We worked it out as part of my departure; we agreed to say it was a restructure." So Ashley and her supervisor got their stories straight, avoiding blame and negative feelings in their public statements. Of course there were hard feelings and challenges working out the separation, but to their peers and the industry, it appeared to be professionally handled.

Karen was let go from a senior-level position after two years of service. "My boss was new and didn't think I was a fit with the new leadership. I kept my composure and remained calm and positive. I asked him if we could agree to say that my departure was part of the organization's leadership transition. He agreed and said I was a 'classy lady.' Then the company crafted a positive e-mail to the employees, which listed many of my accomplishments and thanked me for my service. I was sad to lose this great job, but I have no ill will toward the company. And I keep in touch with many of my former coworkers."

After twelve years with her organization, Stacy was told she would be losing her position. She had a new boss who didn't think she was working up to speed. She was given a month's notice before she had to leave.

Stacy kept her calm, and they both agreed to say she was retiring early. Stacy remained level-headed during the conversation and then stepped outside to call her husband and process what just happened. The company provided Stacy advance notice, and she continued to work for the next three months. She stuck to their story and made a strong effort to guide her coworkers. Later her supervisor commented that her professionalism was noticed and appreciated.

Most people can read between the lines and understand that the departure was not voluntary. The point is not to deceive, but rather to demonstrate goodwill. More specifically, for the employer the point is to preserve good relations with the existing employees who may fear for their own positions. It also demonstrates to employees that the employer is taking the high road. For the person leaving, it preserves his or her dignity and provides the person with recognition for his or her work. And again, it is far better than a sterile "Effective today, John Smith is no longer with us" announcement.

## Exits Without a Strategy

It is true that some departures do not lend themselves to an exit strategy. In some cases, employees break the law, are under the influence, steal, harass, or commit some egregious act. They have violated policy such that their departure must be immediate. That can leave others wondering what happened. And employers are encouraged by their legal counsel not to divulge reasons for termination. Without knowing the facts, they may blame the employer.

Yet, when possible, it is advisable for both the company and the employee to agree on an exit story. Consider these examples from the headlines that demonstrate that without an agreed-upon statement, the organization and the employee can be harmed.

In chapter 3 is a description of Ann Curry's painful and public departure from the *Today* show. Ann delivered her own exit story on national television, one that was obviously not done in partnership with her employer. Brian Stelter of the *New York Times* reported, "Her tearstained departure from *Today* had become a public relations debacle, deeply damaging the most lucrative franchise in television news. Just one day after Curry signed off, the advantage *Today* had over its top rival, ABC's *Good Morning America,* turned into a 600,000 viewer deficit. Millions in advertising revenue vanished. On particularly bad days, *Good Morning America* beat *Today* by a million viewers. Some of this was attributed to Curry's fans exacting revenge...And more than any other show, *Today* had sold itself as a family—America's First Family."

For Ann Curry the departure had a devastating impact. Stelter reported in his article, "If the network was still reeling from her mismanaged departure, Curry, who spent much of the past year lying low at her home in New Canaan, Connecticut, had not yet recovered, either. She still often woke before dawn as if she were about to go on the air. Some mornings, she cried as she read e-mail and Twitter messages from fans. For weeks she couldn't bring herself to return to 30 Rock, where her closed office door bore a red Post-it note that read 'Do Not Enter' in capital letters...She was overwhelmed by condolences. 'It feels like I died,' she told colleagues afterward, 'and I've seen my own wake.'"

This poorly managed departure worked to the disadvantage of the employer and the employee. And while this was a high-profile media event, poorly managed departures can cause damage.

Here is another example as told through various media sources in Pittsburgh:

In 2013 turnovers occurred in four high-level positions at The Heinz Endowments in Pittsburgh. Robert Vagt announced his resignation as president of The Heinz Endowments following the departures of the vice president of finance and administration, the senior director of the environmental program, and the communications director.

The publicity resulting from the lack of an exit story created concern in the community. "When four senior-level managers all leave in the matter of months, you would be a fool not to wonder what was going on. Could it be coincidental? Sure, but unlikely," said Laura Otten, executive director of the Nonprofit Center at La Salle University in Philadelphia.

In the *TribLive* online article "Heinz Staff Shift Linked to Chief's Son," Bill Zlatos and Debra Erdley interviewed community members about their reaction to the terminations. "It's unsettling when someone so established is uprooted like that, so I would imagine it's demoralizing," a nonprofit leader said. "I'm sure their attitude is, 'Am I next?'

The lack of an exit story created speculation and unrest in the community the foundation sought to serve. None of the people who left and no one at the foundation commented on the cause of the departures. Confidentiality of the employer and the employee is the norm. This protects the organization as well as the employee. And yet, nature abhors a vacuum. Speculation fills the void. An agreed-upon exit story would also fill that void.

While most departures don't hit the media, without an agreed-upon exit story, the organization, its employees, and the individual—and occasionally the community—can be hurt.

In Alexa's case, no one at the company even acknowledged her departure. "When I left, no one on my team acknowledged that I left. No one said goodbye. Not one person said, 'I'm sorry, good luck.' Terrible, terrible experience. I had to be the one to say I'm sorry it didn't work out. I shouldn't have to walk around and say, 'It's my last day, see you never.'

"I shouldn't have had to say anything. I didn't want to do the walk of shame. I sent an e-mail with project updates. No one asked me the status of any project. No one. They did not care at all. They formed an opinion of me that was inaccurate. They didn't want to talk to me. They didn't want to acknowledge my existence."

In this case, as far as she knows, the only one hurt by this action was Alexa. But she was concerned that her teammates did not want any updates on the projects she was doing for their clients. In addition, she stated, "I am going to reach out to my school and tell them not to send students to that employer anymore. I want someone at the college to know how awfully they handled my exit from the company."

Sometimes it's as simple as timing. My own mother experienced an undignified termination. She worked as a pre-school director for a church. On the last day of school year, she was fired. I came home from high school that day and found her in her room crying. She said the church preschool board wanted to hire a friend of theirs, so they fired her, right before the annual parent-child picnic. The board didn't think she would stay for the picnic, but she did. She said all the parents found out and were upset at the news. As a show of support, they all sat with her at the picnic, while the board and new director sat alone.

Bruce worked as head of a community foundation. He was let go on the opening day of their scholarship awards banquet, but was asked not to say anything until it was over. Bruce refused, "I can't pretend everything is ok." He left the banquet immediately, and the foundation board was in the awkward spot of explaining to the audience why he wasn't there.

Here is another example of a botched termination. Gail reported a poor exit strategy for one of her colleagues. This individual, Jerry, was a nine-year employee in a visible position and known to many in the community. The company decided to perp-walk him out the door one day with no notice or communication. She saw a friend at a fund-raiser who asked her, "What happened to Jerry? To be there one day and out the next—you'd have to think it was a financial or sexual offense. But I know Jerry, and I know neither of those could be true. I guess it just means that your company doesn't know how to fire people."

Mark reported his departure caused disruption and disappointment from his customers and employees. To protest, they wore black armbands to Mark's farewell party. The cake was black. "They weren't mean. It was a sad day for us—to see me go. They wished me success. They figured it out. A former colleague told me, 'I was so mad at you for leaving us. Then I realized it wasn't your choice.'"

Recall how Don was ushered out through the parking lot. "As I walked out to the parking lot, I had a chance to say goodbye to our team; some cried, and many used the word 'railroaded.' I hugged and shook hands with the security guard in tow."

In the news recently was the firing of James Comey as FBI director. He was speaking to his team in California when the televisions in the room began reporting that he had been fired. Someone in the audience saw it and told him. He thought it was a joke, only to find out it was in fact real.

FBI employees were reported to be angry and embarrassed at the poor treatment he received. On the FBI's Family Day in July 2017, in protest, many of the employees wore T-shirts that read, "Comey is my homey." On the back of the T-shirt was a quote from Comey, "We choose to do good for a living." Further, one of the agents, Special Agent Joshua Campbell, wrote an editorial for *USA Today* praising Comey as a "giant of a man with an even bigger heart," citing many of his accomplishments. Special Agent Campbell describes the FBI atmosphere by saying that it "is very much an organization in mourning."

These examples illustrate some negative consequences of a termination that occurs in an insensitive manner without a mutually developed exit story. In her book *Organizational Behavior: Real Research for Real Managers*, Dr. Jone Pearce writes that in addition to the increased likelihood of a wrongful termination suit, the remaining employees will be negatively impacted by an insensitive or undignified departure of a colleague. "Again, remaining employees' judgments about how their co-workers were treated will affect their attitudes toward the organization, their manager and their actions at work." Dr. Pearce continues, "All are watching how the departing employees are treated and asking, Is this a fair organization? They will wonder: If I invest a lot of my time and make commitment to this organization, will I be betrayed or exploited?" Dr. Pearce cautions organizations to weigh the risk of departing employees removing information against the risk of wrongful termination lawsuits, "reduced commitment, increased turnover, and poorer performance produced by treating departing employees as probable criminals."

As said earlier, it is not always possible or even desirable to have both parties collaborate on an exit story. However, if your employer doesn't offer to work with you on one, you may wish to initiate the conversation. Oftentimes it is in both the organization's and the employee's interest to agree on an exit story.

## Finalizing Some Details

One possibility to explore is whether you are eligible for other positions in your company. If you are told your position is being eliminated, or if there are specific layoffs in your area, this may be an option, especially if you are leaving on good terms with your employer.

Margaret worked as an operations manager in a midsize company with several divisions. She knew it was not working out in her current position, and she was negatively associated with a supervisor who she described as unyielding. Instead of terminating Margaret, her employer gave her the opportunity to transfer to another division. They recognized her abilities and her twelve years of service. She chose to stay with the company, and although she took a pay cut, she was able to maintain employment. The company explained that they were just trying to get her to the "right seat on the bus."

Naturally, it doesn't always work this way. After seven years at her company, Julie was told her position was being eliminated. During her termination meeting, she asked about other positions in the company. "I was told I was not being fired but being laid off. So I asked if there were other open positions. They were not willing to look for me." Julie never learned why the company wouldn't assist her in transferring to another position.

If another job in the company isn't possible, part of your exit strategy could be to offer to tie up loose ends with your work. Are there any projects they would like your help with? Would the company like you to do any freelance work for them as part of the transition? While it may be difficult, this offer demonstrates your goodwill and understanding of the company. If you are leaving on good terms, it also might extend your ability to work and create income.

After being encouraged to resign her position, Janice expressed her desire to assist her employer with the transition. She offered to finish up or transfer to someone else any projects she had in the works. Together, she and her employer came up with a list of projects she was to complete before her departure. This served to extend her period of employment and to give her more time to look for a new position.

Obtaining a reference is also something to pursue. If possible, you should ask someone who can speak to your work, preferably a supervisor. It is generally not helpful to ask someone in human resources for a written reference. Those in human resources are reluctant to give references and provide only limited information to those who inquire, due to liability concerns. They will often just report your position and confirm the dates of employment. It is best to talk to your manager or someone else in the company who can vouch for your work or will advocate for you. Ask this person if he or she will serve as a reference for you in the future. You need to secure this as soon as possible. With so many companies requiring online applications, a written reference letter isn't preferable. Online application systems aren't always set up for written references and require instead a list of references before the company will consider an applicant. You will need someone willing to be contacted to give a recommendation by phone or electronically. Unfortunately, this can be an added burden for job seekers.

In addition to someone from work, your external network is another important resource for recommendations. As part of his exit strategy, Wes reached out to the business community in his area. He asked for and received references from those who had done business with him. If your employer or someone at your company won't give you a recommendation, this is an excellent strategy. Business leaders in the community vouched for Wes's competence and integrity.

## The Going-Away Party

> "It was so uncomfortable. They wanted me to
> leave, and they made me sit through a party."
> —JANICE

Sometimes an employer will want to smooth over the firing by offering a goodbye party. This gives the employer a chance to show the other employees that there are no hard feelings and gives the person being let go a chance to say goodbye. It may also be seen as a way of respecting the departing employee.

Stacy's company wanted to acknowledge her accomplishments by throwing a farewell party for her. In particular, her supervisor was appreciative of how professional she acted during the notice period, telling her, "It is noticed." Although she could potentially feel uncomfortable, Stacy agreed to the party since she wanted to provide her employees with some closure and gratitude.

Unlike Stacy, Nick did not want to participate in a going-away party. "On my next visit, my new boss invited me in to the office. 'Hey, I have great news for you. We want to have a going-away party for you to celebrate your fifteen years here.' My response was, 'Thank you, but you eliminated my job. I don't have a job; I don't think it's appropriate to celebrate.' She said, 'That's surprisingly selfish. The party's not about you; it's about everyone working here. They will all feel good that you have a positive departure.' I said, 'I don't see my departure as a happy one.' At that point she said, 'I think we're done.'"

Janice, too, described how her employer insisted on having a party for her. She tried to turn them down, but they persisted. During the party she tried to sit in an inconspicuous place, but they coaxed her to sit at the head of the table. "It was so uncomfortable. They wanted me to leave, and they made me sit through a party."

If you are able to be emotionally calm and show gratitude to your organization, it is good to attend the party. It is a chance for you to say goodbye to your fellow employees. And it does build goodwill. But be prepared for everyone to ask you what your plans are. Have an answer ready. If you are not able to keep a game face on, decline the invitation and ask your closest coworkers to meet with you after work the next week.

## Mind the Gap

As you get off the Tube, the subway in London, you hear an overhead announcement telling you to "mind the gap." This refers to the space or gap between the train door and the landing. The recording urges you to mind the gap, so you don't accidentally put your foot in the gap and fall.

The people interviewed had to mind the gap as well—the time gap on their résumé. In preparing an exit strategy, consider what you will tell future employers. Expect them to ask why you left each position. Expect them to ask you to explain any gaps in your résumé.

Some of the people I interviewed had ready-made exit stories. For example, Andrew could explain his gap by reporting that his position elimination was because of the company's downsizing. Melissa explained that her job loss was due to a new leader's desire to build his own team. Ashley and her boss agreed to say her job loss was due to an organizational restructuring.

Several of the people interviewed could tell potential employers that during their employment gap they were caring for aging parents. Lori explained that she was focusing full time on completing her doctorate degree. Gail, like Lori, told people she was taking a year off to pursue her degree.

Sondra was let go from her first job after college graduation. Since she was there only a few months, she worried about how to explain her short time of employment and the lack of current employment. "I went to my school's career advising office. How do I put this on a résumé? Do I leave it off? I didn't want to because I learned so much. I wanted credit for what I did. My career counselors helped me build a framework for how to explain my getting fired. They gave me clear-cut steps. They told me I could explain that it wasn't a good fit. They encouraged me to talk about what I want moving forward in a job in a way that was productive."

Reaching out to her college career office was an excellent strategy. Sondra was prepared for interview questions about her short stay at her first real job. Having that preparation was a confidence builder for her as well.

If you have a gap on your résumé or need to explain why you left the position abruptly, it is a good idea to develop your own talking points. Your story should be brief, unemotional, and factual—without blaming or bad-mouthing your former employer. Once you develop your "what is the gap" or "why you left" story, practice saying it. Practice and practice until you can say it calmly, nonchalantly, and succinctly, without trying to memorize it. And practice pivoting to what you are looking for and how you think you could be an asset.

An exit story is an important part of an exit strategy. That said, Sondra got her next job by networking. She was hired by someone who knew her. Her exit story wasn't essential because the hiring manager knew her capabilities and her character. She was prepared with an exit story, but because of her networking skills and positive relationships, her story wasn't needed.

## Review Your Options

Bruce spoke of the need to investigate what-if scenarios and develop a course of action. "I wish my wife and I had started the process sooner. There were some other things we needed to talk through. We should have talked sooner. Are we willing to relocate? Are we willing for one of us not to work? So, is your spouse willing to lose his or her job because of your job? You have to go through the list of things. Whose job is more important? Are we willing to be a two-city family? Are we willing to take less salary? Is it reasonable to retire? That's a different mind-set."

"If you decide to retire or not look for another job, what do you need in order to maintain your lifestyle? You get these financial accountants that say you need millions. Why do you need that if your house and cars are paid off? You need to calculate what you need. What can you live on?"

## Have a Plan B

> "Everyone needs a plan. If you are fully employed,
> you should still have a plan B, meaning a
> plan of action in case you lose your job."
> —BRUCE

The people interviewed encourage you to have a plan B, a backup plan. It may be a place you think you could work if you lost your job; it could be a contact you could call on; it may be freelancing or opening your own business. A plan B might involve selling properties or other assets. Or it might be doing something completely different. As Connie said, "I could always work at Chico's if I had to." Bruce advises, "Everyone needs a plan. If you are fully employed, you should still have a plan B, meaning a plan of action in case you lose your job."

Janice had the opportunity to develop her own exit strategy. "Are you going to stay or plan your exit? You have to put your plan together and decide whether you're going to stay or whether you're going to spend a vacation looking for a job while you're still there."

In addition to finding work in the interim, a plan B could also include reducing your expenses. When Randy determined that he would not have his job long term, he sold his house and moved closer to friends and family where he and his wife rented. They intentionally reduced their expenses in anticipation of this job loss. Bruce and his wife sold properties they had accumulated. Elizabeth and her husband drastically cut their expenses when she was fired.

The importance of savings—a rainy-day fund—cannot be overstated. Connie warned, "People have to be on the lookout for themselves; it's easy to get complacent. Things can turn on a dime. I lived on deferred compensation for a year to pay my bills. I took unemployment, and it was only a little spending money. Make sure you have savings or deferred compensation. You need a backup plan for six to twelve months. It bridged me."

Nick knew that a new job for him would likely mean relocation and major change. "The best way to be prepared is to be ready to bounce," he advised.

Having an exit strategy, including a well-rehearsed exit story, will help make an unplanned transition smoother and less severe. With an exit story ready to go, you control what the story is and shape people's perception of you.

## Key Takeaways

1. A termination without an exit story can hurt both the employer and the employee.
2. Consider developing an exit story and strategy while you are employed.
3. With nearly half of new hires failing, it might be good to have an exit strategy when you take a new job. And don't burn bridges with your former employer.
4. Always have a plan B.

# PART 2

## THE RESPONSE AND THE IMPACT

"Being out of work is the greatest danger to your self-esteem. I felt awful. We prayed and prayed about it."

"Shock, sadness, embarrassment. Twelve years later I am still sad about it. I had my ideal position. Sadly, it took a different course. I haven't been in it because someone decided to take it away from me."

"I was determined not to let this define me."

# CHAPTER 7

## FIRE AND RAIN: EMOTIONAL RESPONSES TO LOSING A JOB

> "You can't eat the orange and throw the peel
> away—a man is not a piece of fruit."
> —ARTHUR MILLER, *DEATH OF A SALESMAN*

Fundamentally, a job loss is a loss. On the surface a job loss repre-
sents a loss of income and financial security. That is obvious and
understandable. But the emotional impact of a job loss goes well
beyond the real and actualized fear of lost income. For the people interviewed, jobs were more than a means of income. To them their jobs
and the companies they worked for meant a form of status, a place to
belong, a social network, and a source of self-esteem. The job was a way
to feel useful or creative or to make a difference. When a job is lost, the
impact of that loss can be compounded by the loss of coworkers, income
security, status, purpose, and identity.

Research shows that a job loss can be more painful than the loss of
a spouse through death or divorce. According to the University of East
Anglia and the What Works for Wellness Center, people who are fired
do not return to their prior levels of mental well-being, life satisfaction,
and self-esteem. The British research demonstrated that fired people
will remain unhappy longer while widowed or divorced people return to
their previous state of well-being sooner.

In this study, people willingly shared how losing a job affected them
emotionally. The range of reactions was wide: shock, shame, guilt, fear,

depression, and anger are typical elements of an individual's reaction to losing a job.

This chapter unpacks the emotional experience of job loss by categorizing and describing the types of emotions. Though these are described separately, it is important to understand that these reactions are not mutually exclusive. During the interviews, it was typical for people to jump from one emotion to another. The participants usually experienced multiple emotions or a flood of emotions. In almost *all* cases, the interviewees shared multiple emotions in one powerful statement.

## Shock

> "I, I can't believe this happened. I can't believe this."
> —ELIZABETH

Nearly every person I interviewed with spoke of their tremendous shock over losing their jobs. They admitted that they didn't suspect and weren't prepared for the news. In the interviews, shock was usually the first emotion they reported. (Note: Some were not shocked. In fact they saw the inevitable coming and took a proactive approach to addressing their hunches. I discuss their actions in chapter 5, Fire Escape.) What follows is how four of the participants described their feelings of shock.

In her first job out of college, Sondra admits she missed all the signs of impending job loss. She was heading to work, looking forward to getting assigned her own desk. Up until then she had been sitting at a folding table, so this was to be a big day. Instead, she was called to her boss's office and let go. "I was really blindsided at the time." In Sondra's mind, her company was making a more permanent workstation for her. Being fired was the last thing she expected that morning.

Like Sondra, Alexa also was let go after three months from her first job out of college. She too missed all the signs of impending job loss. "There were ten people on my team. No one talked to each other. I always completed my task on time and got no negative feedback. I had a mentor or supervisor to help me, and she and I were supposed to have standing meetings. I had been trying to meet with her. I wanted to talk with her about someone on my team. This person gave me assignments. She was awful. She gave direction in a confusing and complicated way. She was disorganized. She yelled at me in front of other people.

"I wanted to talk to my supervisor to help make me better communicate with her. I was looking for tips. My supervisor pushed it off—always canceling and rescheduling. Then, when we finally found a time to meet, she asked me to pick out a room for us. We used an office of someone who wasn't there that day.

"I finally got a time to meet with her, and the first thing she says is, 'We need to have a serious conversation. This isn't working out. We are going to let you go.' I was shocked. I walked in with questions, I was prepared, and I brought suggestions to improve communication. I was shocked. I started crying because I wasn't prepared. It was not something I was expecting at all. Still, I thought I was performing well and was doing what I needed to do. Finding out that they had a very different opinion of me than what I thought they had was hard."

Fired after thirteen years with her company, Elizabeth asserted emphatically, "I had no clue I was losing my job. *No clue!* The first day I thought, 'I, I can't believe this happened. I can't believe this.'" Elizabeth had turned in her resignation a few months earlier, but the company begged her to reconsider. She had stayed on, only to be let go.

Nick spoke of his reaction more pensively, "I was in shock. I had devoted my career to this organization. I had come up the ladder with a series of successes. I didn't have a clue. I tried to be positive. It's hard not to be bitter. But if you stay bitter, it just eats you up. My initial reaction was feeling stunned or numb. I think a lot of it for me was grasping the reality: a.) My job was eliminated; b.) I was not going anywhere at the company; and c.) I had to get a new job and would probably have to move." Nick was shocked not only by the job loss, but by what he suspected would be the repercussions of this loss on him and his family.

A lifelong social worker, Brenda described herself as being fired "two and a half times." She shared her reactions passionately, as if she had been fired last week, when in reality her first firing occurred more than ten years prior to the interview. "Out of the blue, shock. I was in shock. I was in total shock—to the point where people were helping me pack my office and load my car. It was awkward. It was terrible. I left. I went to the airport—I commuted to work. Got drunk—straight scotch. Waited for the flight. Sat down at the bar next to some guy. He was a pilot on my flight; he wasn't flying, just a passenger. He said, 'You look like this is the worst day of your life.' I said, 'It is.' I told him what happened. I talked his ear off. We got on the plane. He was last one in; he asked the guy next to me to switch seats. I was literally in shock."

Brenda also described how she felt when she was fired for the second time. Even with prior experience of being let go, she was in shock. "I didn't see it coming. I was in total shock. I walked around the office and said, 'I was just fired.' My boss was new in her job. I had sixteen years in the field; she had four months. I was trying to help her and make her look good." Brenda's shock was amplified because someone with far less experience had fired her.

The shock the interviewees felt came from a couple of places. One, they had received no criticism or negative feedback. In their minds they were doing their jobs well. Another component of their shock was that they felt betrayed. Given no warning and having done nothing wrong, they were shocked that this could happen to them.

## Fear and Stress

> "I lost it. I was so scared."
> —JULIE

Understandably, people voiced concerns about how they would pay their bills or provide for their families. The fear associated with being jobless was primarily related to income insecurity.

Andrew recalled that his first reaction was shock and stress at being let go after sixteen years with the company. Worried about how he would support his wife and two young children, he reassured himself, "I'm sure I will find another job, but besides the Internet, how else will I find a new job?" Andrew had not looked for a job for sixteen years and was unprepared to do so.

A colleague informed Renee that her job was posted online. Renee recalled, "I was sick. I am the breadwinner. I carry the benefits. My husband has a business, but I have the steady income and benefits. We live in a small town. There isn't another company I could move to. It made me sick. I didn't know what to do." Like Andrew, Renee was the main provider for her family and carried the health insurance benefits. Also like Andrew, she hadn't looked for a new job in years. Living in a small town, Renee's fear was compounded because she was unable to relocate without uprooting her husband's business.

At thirty, Julie was let go after seven years of service to her company. As a young mother, she worried about supporting her family. "I lost it. I was so scared. A whole wave of emotion. I was worried about how I would provide for my one-year-old daughter. Groceries, bills, the house. I am the breadwinner. I thought I was there for the long haul." Julie's fears were realized as she withdrew from her retirement account to pay the mortgage and eventually had to file for bankruptcy. Job loss is understandably one of the leading causes of bankruptcy.

Sondra felt the stress of unemployment immediately. Her first job allowed her to launch herself with an apartment in the city and a car. "People didn't know what to do with me because I was so stressed out. I had a new apartment, a car payment, and my first student loan payment was coming due. Bank account empty and credit card maxed out."

## Guilt

> "No matter how long I live, I will never forgive myself
> for moving him his senior year. I just feel so bad."
> —DON

A few of the respondents experienced guilt in relation to losing their jobs. The guilt was not associated with their performance at work or feeling that they should have done something to prevent their job loss. Rather, the guilt was associated with the consequences that their being fired had on their families.

Having to move to another state to find comparable employment, Nick carries feelings of guilt and regret that he's not back home and able to help his parents. The married father of two shared, "On my bad days,

I feel like I failed and let my family down. None of them have given me any reason to think that. But I am not available to help my parents and my family back home. My mom tells me about issues I could help with if I were still at my old organization. But I can't now. She says, 'We wish you were there.' I know. That's what I haven't been able to let go of."

Like Nick, Don described with great sorrow how his family had to relocate so he could find work. While being interviewed, he often sighed, looked down, and shook his head. "I finally got a job out here. We are so grateful. But I feel awful to have had to move my family. My kids were doing so well in school, and we had to move them. We prayed about it. Two of them in high school, one going away to college. Poor Connor, we moved him his senior year. No matter how long I live, I will never forgive myself for moving him his senior year. I just feel so bad. When I was a kid, my dad moved us frequently, and I said I would never do that to my kids. And here we moved in his last year of high school. I feel just awful. I know we had to do it, and I am grateful for this job, but I feel so guilty."

## Devastated

> "I was devastated. I thought I had no value."
> —BRENDA

*Devastated* is the second most commonly used word that the participants used to describe their reaction to being fired. *Merriam-Webster's Collegiate Dictionary*, ninth edition, defines *devastate* as to destroy much or most of (something); to cause great damage or harm to (something); to cause (someone) to feel extreme emotional pain. Each of these definitions reflects the feelings experienced after being fired. The interviewees felt that their lives were destroyed or harmed and that they were caused extreme emotional pain.

After bringing in a big client to her consulting firm, Kate was let go. "I was so devastated. I had just pulled in this major account. But I decided I would never put my career in someone else's hands again. I started my own business, and it's tough, but I am going to make it. Never let someone else carry your ball."

Recall that Brenda was terminated on three different occasions. After being let go the first two times, Brenda remembered, "I was devastated. I thought I had no value. But anyway, I gave both companies my blood, sweat, and tears." Describing the third time she was fired, she said, "I was so devastated. I was the first executive in the company's history to develop a successful fund-raising event. It was incredible, a big hit with the community."

Diane shared a painful picture of being devastated. "It was awful; I was so hurt. I had worked there my whole life. I started many of their programs. I gave everything. It was the hardest thing I have been through. It was who I was. I identified with the company. I identified with the mission. I compare it to divorce and death. Twenty-eight years. It was horrible. Well, I loved all those people, I loved the customers, I loved the staff—it was my baby. I built it from the ground up. I loved that I felt good at it. I know I can do this well. I miss feeling competent."

## Depression

> "The depression of sitting around
> not working is exhausting."
> —MARK

As with other losses, depression is a common emotional response to losing a job. A study by the Pew Research Center found that the long-term unemployed are significantly more likely to say they sought professional help for depression or other emotional issues while out of work (24 percent versus 10 percent for those unemployed less than three months).

A job loss is more than just a loss of income. Job loss can also mean a loss of activity, status, community, and identity. Profound losses may turn from normal grief to depression. The people I interviewed shared how depression affected them after losing a job.

For example, Julie became so depressed that it was too difficult for her to talk about her job loss. "I had to stop talking to people about it. I am trying to put this behind me. I lost a couple friends doing that. I guess they weren't my friends. There is a huge cut on your character, and it does darken your spirit. Society puts so much on your character." As an act of self-preservation, Julie had to distance herself from people who continued to want to talk to her about the details of her job loss while she was trying to cope and move on.

Sharing his painful emotional journey, Mark reflected, "I went through all the feelings. Lost. Scared. All the emotions. But anytime there is a long pause between jobs, it is lonely and depressing. Then my wife got me a dog. She was intuitive in finding me stopgaps. I do best when I am helping others. When I could take care of neighbors, I would help them. Then I had surgery—that took up time. But surgery intensified the depression. That was terrible. I put off surgery for seven years because I was a loyal employee. Well, here I am, no job. Now I can have it done."

Not only was Mark's depression compounded by the pain and recovery of surgery, it was also exacerbated when he would lament his decision to leave a good job where he was successful for the company that fired him. "It made me appreciate longevity with a job. In my old job, I always could grow. It was fun to take on new opportunities. In the end when I left that job, I felt I had done everything. I needed a new challenge. Those are the times depression sets in. I had it so good in my old job, why did I leave?"

Mark profoundly states, "The depression of sitting around not working is exhausting."

After losing her position, Melissa also became depressed. She sought answers and continued to ask herself why, after being so successful, she was let go. For her the depression was founded in her shattered belief that hard work and success would be rewarded. "I went into a depression. I couldn't logically think of why it happened. There was no logic. You go through the stages. Tears at first, then you are so isolated because your work was so much."

Depression also overwhelmed Joe, who compared his job loss to death. "I turned inside. Even though initially I didn't acknowledge it, I became depressed. It was like a death. The other thing was, my dad died two years earlier and things came back. I got depressed. I used outplacement services. The rooms were filled with white males my age or older-seventy-five to one hundred guys looking for work. I was competing against them. I was depressed seeing so many and hearing how long they were out of work. I got more depressed, turning inward, being despondent. I thought, 'I have all this to offer.' The feeling of rejection—I didn't cope well. It was a death.

Losing my job was a death. Even to this day, I have a better appreciation. I can relate that losing my job was like a death. I kept it inside of me until I realized I needed to get outside and start talking to others. Going through denial. I thought I had to be tough, keep a stiff upper lip, and verbalize that all is well—when it wasn't."

## Shame, Loss of Self-Esteem, Embarrassment

"I was so sad, I felt useless. I was ashamed."
—ASHLEY

Shame, embarrassment, and loss of self-esteem were also common emotional reactions to losing a job. This finding was validated by the Pew Research Center. Their 2010 study found that, not surprisingly, loss of self-respect was an outcome of job loss: 38 percent of the long-term unemployed, those unemployed more than six months, reported losing some self-respect while out of work, compared with 29 percent who were jobless less than three months.

The phrase *loss of self-respect* conveys a degree of emotion. But from the participants in my interviews, you can see how poignant and painful this emotion really is.

Don, who was let go less than a year of winning a major company award, said simply, "Being out of work is the greatest danger to your self-esteem. I felt awful. We prayed and prayed about it."

After losing her job, Ashley felt shame. "I was so sad, I felt useless. I was ashamed. I didn't think anyone wanted to talk to me. I was so upset. I left a great job to come to this company. Then my boss retired. 'How could you do this to me?' I wanted to stay, but I knew my new boss would want to pick his own team. I felt so terrible. I just wanted to hide. I couldn't talk to anyone."

Describing her feelings of shame and loss of self-esteem, Melissa revealed, "I felt like a pariah. I don't know the cure for gaining your confidence back. I don't know that cure. It took me a long time to get it back. I was always told you work hard, you add money to the bottom line, and you get rewarded. That myth was blown out of the water."

So embarrassed over being fired, Lori explained that she would avoid seeing people from work, which was difficult in a small town. "On the occasion I would see someone, I was so embarrassed. Like at the grocery store, I would duck in another aisle to avoid seeing anyone from work. I knew I had nothing to be ashamed of, but I was embarrassed. I was the exemplar of management; I was a high achiever. I was so embarrassed, even though I knew it was a lie."

Mark shared his darkest moments: "After surgery I spent so much time in bed, crying, 'Why am I upset? What's wrong with me?' In adulthood it's a well-known fact that we find our value in things we are needed for or things we do. We take our value from those. I was experiencing a loss of value."

Let go within her first ninety days of her dream job, Theresa wrote, "I am so ashamed. I let everyone down." She left another position to come to an organization she respected and admired. Two employees on the inside advocated for her and served as her references.

## Anger

> "It's like a divorce."
> —BRUCE

For two people, anger was directed at how their termination was compounded by mechanisms in place to greatly reduce their future employment choices.

In her late fifties, Rhonda was asked to step down from a position she held for eight years in public service. "It was unexpected. And I couldn't say anything. I was restricted from working in my field for a year. I was so angry. I didn't know I could be so angry. And I didn't know how to relax. I really couldn't just relax. That worried me. I mean, what will I do in retirement?"

Melissa shared her anger. "I was so angry. They wanted me to sign an agreement where I would get my vacation pay and a very small severance if I agreed to a noncompete. I called a lawyer, but I couldn't sign it. She told me, 'You have no right to work.' The bottom line is nothing protects the job of a manager."

Sondra's anger was borne out of a sense of unfairness. "It took time. I was angry, more angry than depressed. I was trying. I didn't deserve to be fired. I was out of work for three months on unemployment. It was intense," Sondra shared.

"I was really upset about it, and especially the way it was done," recalled Wes. His employer accused him of wrongdoing but would not tell Wes what they believed he did. Nor was Wes permitted to address accusations. "I talked to a couple attorneys to see if there were actions I could take. Having been in finance, I knew the company's severance practices. Every situation prior to mine, we were generous with a severance, but I was offered nothing. The attorney said they were not willing to do anything."

Like Wes, Lori dealt with false accusations. "Depression, yes, and I was angry, but not at any one person. I wanted to be angry at people, but I couldn't. My compassion won over the anger. It was more about being angry at the situation and the unfairness. I always prided myself on being fair, on listening to others. I was angry at the system especially, as someone who is used to being a problem solver. You can't enact your skill set for yourself. They wouldn't allow me to fix it. You are left being so incomplete."

While Lori became angry at the situation and the unfairness, Bruce directed his anger at his boss. "Initially I have to process things. 'OK, I expected this.' It doesn't feel good. I got more emotional over time, especially when colleagues, members, and friends offered support. But it was hard not to direct anger at my boss. It's like a divorce. It was hard for me to say this; if you've been through a divorce, you'll understand. It's not the person; we have a difference of opinion. I don't have any ill feelings anymore, but it takes a while. Sometimes they come back.

"In my view there are lots of options—especially when you consider taking away someone's livelihood. It's hard enough to get a job, but much harder when you are sixty-one. People don't want to hire you when you're sixty-one."

"There was some anger in there," Mark admitted. "It was hard. It was minimized because I didn't value the values of that company. Theirs were less than mine as far as how people should be treated. I was putting myself in a bubble and separating myself from the corruption. I wanted to be my own boss and make my own decisions. In most cases I did. I quickly got over feeling less of a professional because I didn't feel that they were professional.

"My trust, my faith, says to be obedient and faithful and good things come to you. With life-altering events like divorce, you think, 'This is incredulous, I can't believe it's happening.' I told people I was forced to resign. It felt like a divorce."

Families too expressed their anger. Barbara said she became livid when her husband was let go in a very pubic manner after many years of service with his company. "My husband went into a dark depression. He was so ashamed and sad. This was his whole life. And they cast a cloud over him when they shared the news. I was angry; I had to fight for him because he couldn't fight for himself." More family reactions are included in the following chapter.

## Reflection

Some of the study's participants reflected on their experiences, trying to understand and learn from them. For example, Mark questioned himself, "I wonder what I could have done differently. There is a part of me that knows I was good."

Looking back, Randy also tried to figure out if there was anything else he could have done to change the course of things. "I do have times when I wonder what I could have done differently to change the outcome, but after much thinking, I don't think there are any actions I could have taken that would have resulted in me staying, given the fact that none of the other key players were changing."

## Disillusionment

> "There are no real happy endings."
> —MELISSA

Many of the people interviewed became disillusioned with employment after their job loss. According to a study by the Pew Research Center, losing a job is not just a blow to the pocketbook.

According to the survey, nearly half (46%) of those who lost a job recently agreed that "success in life is pretty much determined by forces outside our control," a view shared by only about a third of other Americans (34%). About three-quarters agree with the view that "the rich just get richer while the poor get poorer," a sentiment expressed by two-thirds of other adults. The recently jobless are also 9 percentage points more likely to believe that most rich people today are wealthy because of personal connections or family money, and not as a result of their own hard work. Americans who lost a job in the previous year also are somewhat more likely to be dissatisfied with the direction of the country as a whole (72% vs. 61%).

"Who would have thought?" Connie questioned, expressing her dismay at losing a job after twenty-eight years. "People are just bad news. Not everyone thinks about what's good for the company. They want to get rid of people. If they are secure, they like people who are competent who make them look good. If they are insecure, they have to get rid of that person."

Animated and angry, Melissa described her sense of betrayal. "My God, the story that they tell you—work hard, do a good job, and you'll be rewarded—is a myth. It's crazy. Employment at will is the reality. I will never seek out the big job, the big title, again. I just want a job now. If you achieve, then everyone achieves, but that's not it; people don't see it that way. Employment at will—who's will? Not mine! There are no real happy endings."

Joe lamented, "I felt betrayed. I was raised that hard work, being loyal, and treating others with respect would be rewarded. That didn't pan out. You can be doing the best job and be successful, but for reasons beyond your control you can lose your job. The counselors say look at this as an opportunity. Something is always positive. I can tell you it's not an opportunity."

Losing a job created feelings of disillusionment and betrayal. No longer did people believe their success was in their control, but rather more due to factors outside their control. Allison Pugh, author of *The Tumbleweed Society*, describes this as the one-way honor system.

The one-way honor system is when individual workers profess having an intense work ethic that also involves loyalty or identifying with the employers. Many people that I interviewed said that they give "150 percent, or 100 percent, or 125 percent," so the individual is pledging themselves as a statement of personal character. They're saying, "I'm a good person, see how much I identify with work and can be relied on."

"On the other hand, for the last 30 years or so, employers have been pulling away from making any similar pledge. And there's no blame for employers—even people who had been laid off said it's not the company's job to worry about workers, they have to be lean and mean in a tough economy. Americans appear to have entirely capitulated to the model of the high-performance company that doesn't owe anything to workers aside from, as one woman that I interviewed said, "a paycheck and some respect."

Disillusionment, dismay, and betrayal were common reactions as participants experienced at the one-way honor system. It's like they were saying, "I'm a good person, I did a good job, I worked hard. I did what I was supposed to. But that didn't matter."

## Resignation or Acceptance

> "All right, God, what do you want me to do? I
> surrender. I will do whatever you want."
> —BRENDA

The participants described how they accepted or became resigned to their circumstances. Initially, Mark tried to make the best of it. "At first, in talking to my friends, I didn't take it personally. I said, 'Congratulate me on entering the next chapter of my life.' I tried to be positive." Mark's attempt to be positive and not to take things personally didn't last. Once the reality of his situation set in, Mark admitted he was incredulous and that it felt like a divorce. Mark put on a good attitude at first, trying to accept his situation and be positive, but reality eventually sank in, and he was deeply affected by anger and depression. Mark returned to acceptance as his career in consulting took off and he became successful at his own business.

Taking a pragmatic approach, Janice said, "That's real life. I didn't think about it before. But no job is the same all the time. Things change. That's my motto. I don't know, sometimes I think we could have the same thing at my new job, but we couldn't. We had something special. It is what it is."

"Nothing lasts forever. Things change. It's tough," Connie said in a matter-of-fact manner.

Elizabeth called on her faith to build acceptance for her situation. "I remember going to church the first Sunday after I was let go. I met with the ladies. They all gathered around me. I told them I was let go. They were all concerned: 'Oh no! Not you!' And so on. I told them, 'I know God has something better for me. I am OK. I don't want you to be disappointed because I am let go. I am OK with it.'"

After her third experience being fired from a job, Brenda became resigned to her situation. "After I got the news, I went home and told my husband. And then I sat on my chair in the living room and said, 'All right, God, what do you want me to do? I surrender. I will do whatever you want.' And I just sat."

Brenda shared that she intently looked for direction: "I had time to think, get quiet. I got a chance to listen—wherever the messages came from. It's not people telling you what to do. It's listening to your own heart, mind. That's where I was able to admit the job was a big stressor. I don't know if I would have had the courage to quit. This forced me to take another pass. Is this almost divine intervention? Does it allow you to take another pass? When the door shuts, a window opens. It allowed me to really look at this: What am I to learn, and where am I to go?"

Gaining acceptance for Diane meant recognizing the need to forgive: "I had to forgive them, or I would be very bitter. I realized I did what I did for the people I served. They couldn't take that from me. I had done what I had done out of love. 'I won't forget what I did for love'; that's my song," referring to a song from *A Chorus Line*.

## PTFD: Post-Traumatic Firing Disorder

"I hate that feeling! 'Let's go into a room'—panic!"
—SONDRA

Some of the people I met admitted to revisiting painful emotions despite trying to move forward. Bitterness, anger, and fear can resurface. Overreaction is also common.

It took Paul three years to find full-time work after being let go. He was able to do some consulting work but needed to work full time. He described starting his new job: "I got another job. My boss gave me some feedback, and I freaked out. I know I'm not confident. I had such a bad experience after getting fired. It took a long time to get a full-time job. Now that I have one, I find myself looking over my shoulder. When I get feedback, I imagine I am going to get fired again." Paul braces himself for the worst, even though he is successfully employed again.

Likewise, Sondra said, "Even though I feel really good about where I am, I always look over my shoulder now. I get freaked out when my boss says, 'We should grab a room.' That was the trigger for me. 'Let's meet in the conference room.' I panic inside. Now they actually want to meet with me for legitimate reasons, like to discuss revenue targets or budgets. But I always panic. *I hate that feeling!* 'Let's go into a room'—*panic!*"

Sondra reported overcompensating at her new job. "I'm always working so hard so they can't say anything about my work. I don't want them to have anything to use against me."

Even after twelve years, Lori remains affected by being fired. "Shock, sadness, embarrassment. Twelve years later I am still sad about it. I had my ideal position. Sadly it took a different course. I haven't been in it because someone decided to take it away from me." She marked the twelve-year anniversary of losing her job on social media: "It's been twelve years since I left employment from a job I loved. I'm still trying to find my place, but it's good to know that victory is mine through Christ."

Don is haunted not only by his own job loss but his father's as well. "I wonder if I have become my father; he left a very secure position at a scientific center in the shadow of Stanford University to join one of Silicon Valley's many start-up companies. It tanked. He spent the remainder of his life bouncing from company to company. Eventually he died in abject poverty. His account didn't even have the funds to bury him, so we had to come up with the money to do so. And I am different now. I give 125 percent every day so our company can be successful. I will do whatever it takes."

Despite becoming employed again and making an effort to move on, the respondents maintain some remnants of these emotions, and they resurface on occasion.

Conducting these interviews, and this section specifically, was difficult for both the interviewer and the participants. By answering my questions, the interviewees had to revisit the difficult emotions of sadness, anger, and disillusionment. Thanks to their openness, the emotional trauma of losing a job is vividly described and hopefully better understood.

## Key Takeaways

1. A job loss is a loss. In addition to loss of income, there is also a loss of security, status, self-esteem, and the social support and activity of work.
2. Once people lose a job, they may continue to be fearful and haunted by the experience even when they get another job.
3. Coming to terms with the job loss and moving on is difficult. Professional help or support groups may be beneficial.
4. Losing a job can be just as painful as losing a spouse.

# CHAPTER 8

## FRIENDLY FIRE AND FIRE'S WARMTH: FINDING OUT WHO YOUR REAL FRIENDS ARE

This chapter continues the discussion about the impact of job loss on the person fired, as well as the effect on his or her family and friends. One of the most surprising things that happened after the job loss itself was how it changed the person's relationships with people whom he or she considered to be friends. On top of losing income security and the status related to being employed, many people described the disappointment they felt in how their friends treated them. Friendships abandoned and friendships strengthened are described in this chapter, beginning with the stories of friendly fire—the friends who turned away from those who lost their jobs.

### Friendly Fire

In divorce the support of friends is essential—likewise in a job loss. And as in a divorce, it often happens that friends take sides. In job loss, friends from work also might believe they need to take sides. The interviewees described how they felt betrayed and disappointed by some of their friends. Friendly fire came in several forms: fear, avoidance, reopening the wound, and outright betrayal.

# Fear

> "It's like they have to choose between
> contacting you and keeping their jobs."
> —MELISSA

Brenda shared her disappointment about a friend and coworker's lack of support: "Word spread through the rumor mill like lightning. Nine-thirty in the morning. Nothing was said to my staff. I am being escorted out of the building." Her friend, the vice president of human resources, apologized over and over. 'Where was your spine? I asked. If you are so sorry, why didn't you stand up for me?' She said, 'I didn't want to be fired.'" Fear prevented her from advocating for Brenda.

That fear is not unusual. Sometimes people feel their own jobs are at risk if they contact someone who was let go. Melissa said, "I felt like a pariah. Friends at work couldn't talk to me. The company watched phone calls and e-mails; they could monitor everything. I didn't want to get anyone in trouble, the people I worked with day in and day out. It's like they have to choose between contacting you and keeping their jobs. It was like a divorce where people had to choose whether they were friends with the husband or the wife. That contributed to my depression."

Paula explained this dynamic: "People are afraid of contacting you after you are let go. They are afraid if they contact the person who was fired, the company will see them as disloyal. They know that it can happen to anyone. People are afraid for their own jobs. And even when they want to reach out, people don't know what to say.

"When I was fired, I wrote a letter to one of my staff members. The letter was to thank her for her great work and to tell her how talented she was and how I wished her well. I didn't get a response. I e-mailed her once again, but this person who I worked so closely with never acknowledged my letter. She never even checked to see how I was doing."

While she was still employed, Lesley sought out the advice of a close colleague. "Do you know how HR is treating me?" she asked. He said, "I do." Lesley then asked, "Why is it being allowed?" He answered, "I adore you, but I can't jeopardize my job for you."

Sometimes a company explicitly forbids its employees from contacting someone who has been fired. Lori remarked sadly, "The thing that hit me was I was never able to say goodbye to my people; I couldn't say goodbye. They were my team. We were thirty-six people. They were told they were not allowed to contact me. It was a gag order—ridiculous."

## Avoidance

> "But no one still working there called
> to ask how I was doing."
> —JANICE

Bruce talked about the disappointment he felt when people he thought were friends didn't reach out. "I had advocates, but there were also people who I'd helped who were very negative. And they wouldn't be where they are if it weren't for my help. I got someone on a board and recommended someone else for his current job. *I guess I am surprised at who doesn't call.* I would have thought Eric would have helped. I sent him an e-mail and didn't hear from him. I thought he was a friend. That was the most troubling."

Similarly, Janice recalled, "Most of the people I worked with said they were sorry I was leaving. After I left, others who were fired before me came out of the woodwork. But no one still working there called to ask how I was doing."

Describing how quickly a friend turned on him, Nick recounted, "There was a guy at work. We are neighbors; our daughters were classmates. As soon as the word was out that I was a marked man, he wouldn't make eye contact. I came down a hallway and saw him coming out of the elevator. I waved and said hi. He just avoided eye contact with me and walked away. I mean, we are neighbors; I thought we were friends. Don't I take your daughter to soccer practice? That tells you about who those people are. They are people I don't need to spend time thinking about or worrying about. Bad things will happen, and you have to deal with them. Put them in the past."

In addition to his friend, Nick recalled, "The person at the top couldn't make eye contact. Had he just been honest, I would have appreciated his honesty. Instead, he pretended he was my advocate but then wouldn't say he'd support my efforts to get another job in the organization."

Lori was disappointed that the head of her company avoided her. "The real interesting thing is the retiring CEO didn't back me up. He didn't want to get involved. Now he is on Facebook with me and is kind of like a grandpa to me. It may be his way of making amends. I think he regrets it."

## Betrayal

> "For Lila to cut me off at the knees was so hurtful."
> —JULIE

Several of the people I interviewed felt betrayed by someone in their company. Often it was someone they considered a friend.

For example, Gail shared how she helped a good friend get a job, only to be betrayed by her: "A good friend of mine was fired and just leaving her position. We had been friends for years. She was at my wedding; I was at her birthday parties. I suggested that she apply for a job with us. I was the matchmaker. She would not have gotten the job without me. The boss had another candidate. I persuaded him to go with her.

"After she started working, I pushed back on one of her ideas. We couldn't afford to do it. That was my kiss of death. And I knew it as soon as I said it. I knew it was dangerous. I remember having a meeting with her and our boss where the two of them called me on the carpet for something stupid. I knew it was a cover for what was going on. She was going to the boss saying I had to go.

"The more she saw the influence I had inside and outside the organization, the more I became a threat to her. That dynamic intensified over time. It became them against me. So I knew something was up during my leave because neither one of them was in touch with me at all.

"All of that combined was the beginning of the end."

Being close friends with the boss can be especially challenging. Julie became good friends with her supervisor, Lila. The company was having financial troubles, and despite Lila's regular assurances that her job wasn't in jeopardy, Julie was let go. "I received a visit from Lila at the end of the day. She made small talk; she was nervous. She got four glasses of water in twenty minutes. She kept saying how her boss was stressing her out. She pretended to get a text. 'Speak of the devil; she wants to see you in the human resources office.' I asked, 'What's going on? Am I getting fired?' 'Julie, you're not getting fired, you didn't do anything,' she answered. I walked out of my office and into HR. They shut the door. At that moment I thought they were telling me that Lila was getting fired and I was getting her job. Lila's boss mentioned that there were budget cuts and that they needed to eliminate a position. And then she said, 'It's going to be you.'

"Lila wasn't performing up to par, so at first I thought I was being promoted to her position. I was blindsided. It made me angry that Lila was going to take over my duties. It made me angry.

"I rushed back to my area and found Lila. I confronted her. 'You are a liar. You knew what was going on.' She replied, 'I didn't lie.' Then she knew I knew. 'Oh Julie, I didn't know how to handle it.' I said, 'You've got me out of your way now.' She realized I was serious. She left.

"Lila and I had been friends. We spent a lot of time together talking about our private lives. We were Facebook friends. It hurt even worse since she lied to me. It was so hurtful. We had become friends and allies. We helped each other. She so betrayed me. It shook me to my core. It made me angry, more at her than the company. The company had been so good to me. So many opportunities were given to me. For Lila to cut me off at the knees was so hurtful."

## Reopening the Wound

"I had to stop talking to people about it."

—JULIE

Sometimes friends of the participants continued to bring up unpleasant memories. Mark explained how his former coworkers made it difficult for him to move on. "I have stayed in touch with many of them, but it's not in my best interest because I didn't want to hear things that were happening at the company. It made me feel helpless and bad for them. It's like the Job parable, but they say all the wrong things. They thought I wanted to hear all the things that went wrong. I didn't. That was my legacy. Then I didn't want to go out and eat with them."

Like Mark, Julie had challenges with friends after she lost her job. "People called all the time, so the wound stayed open and never got to heal. 'Oh my God, what happened,' they'd ask. I thought I was there for the long haul. I had to stop talking to people about it. I am trying to put this past me. I lost a couple friends doing that. I guess they weren't my friends."

## Family Furor

If friendly fire was lobbed at the interviewees from some of their friends, none reportedly came from family members. Not one of the interviewees indicated that a family member blamed them or was angry at them. For the most part, families were supportive and strongly defended their loved ones. They even expressed anger and resentment toward the company. Families seemed to have lived through their loved ones' struggles and commitments at work and were often relieved that they no longer had to endure the challenge.

However, Joe acknowledged, "It was very tough on our marriage. My wife likes stability, being in control, and knowing what's going on. She didn't have control. She didn't know where she and the kids were going to be. She was trying to think about the kids and me when I wasn't being strong and stable. It was very stressful."

## Relief, Compassion, and Anger

> "They're assholes; they don't deserve you!"
> —DEREK, MELISSA'S HUSBAND

After Gail lost her job of fifteen years, her family was relieved that she would no longer have to work at her company. "My family was very happy, tired of watching me overfunction for the organization for so many years. They had complete faith in me and my resilience. They were also angry at the 'how' and actually have not forgiven them." When Janice was asked to leave after fifteen years, her family had a similar reaction. "My family was 'rah rah' because they knew I was so upset. They'd say, 'If they aren't treating you right, then you don't need to be there.' They also couldn't understand it, 'How could you have worked all those hours and done all that good and they not appreciate you?' It was very hard for them to grasp. They couldn't understand how it could happen."

Bob was shocked and angry at the news of his wife, Connie, being fired from her law firm. "Those people are idiots. You don't take a twenty-eight-year employee and throw her on the streets. You don't do that." Bob, several years older than Connie, had been thinking of retiring. He said, "I will just wait." He called the firing retaliatory and political. Connie told her husband: "It had nothing to do with the fact clients liked me, liked my work. I was the only one who tried an actual case." Bob responded, "They're idiots."

Randy described how his wife responded to the news of his departure. He had anticipated that he would be fired and worked out a departure with his boss. "My wife is pretty intuitive; she was living it same as I was. She was supportive in making the change and thought I should do it sooner. Afterward, I told friends and family I was making the change, that I wasn't getting what I wanted. I was worried about feedback, what they'd say.

"I didn't check with anyone other than my wife. That helped. I didn't have to worry about their reactions. People think you have to get another job quick. It's a long process. People have noticed a big difference in me already. Right now I am OK."

Randy cautioned that it's important to have solid family relationships before encountering a job loss: "Family support has to be built before the deep water struggling begins."

"I called my wife right away," Mark related. "She knew I felt something was going on—'something's not right.' My wife stood right by me. She stood by. That was a relief. She said, 'Here's your chance to move into consulting quicker.' We are fortunate. I told friends of ours, but I didn't say anything to anyone else."

Elizabeth was let go from her job just months after her company begged her to stay. "I got in the car and called my husband. He said, '*No way!* All the hours you worked for the company. All you put in.' He was very upset. I never told my mom because of her stroke. She never knew because I was busy with my consulting."

"I went home and waited for my husband, Derek," Melissa shared. "I told him, and he of course goes into the macho, 'They're assholes; they don't deserve you!' Talk about my husband—he has never met a stranger. He has gotten me to meet people at the university. He knows someone at an insurance company, not that she could get me a job, but she could elevate my application. He brought home a business card of someone else. He said, 'Call her up.' He is doing networking for me while I am trying to get my bearings. I am so guarded."

Nick recalled that when he lost his job, his family "was great—sympathetic and supportive. My daughter could have been moody, unpleasant, and bitchy. It was her senior year. She gave me a big hug. We spent tons of time together, and it was great. We made the most out of it.

"My wife from day one said, 'As long as I am with you, I am home. We have a family.' We moved here and had a great Thanksgiving. But she was very angry and still is. She hasn't forgiven them. She still has her voodoo doll."

"I called my daughter at college to tell her I had lost the job," Mona shared. "She burst out crying. She knew everyone I worked with. She'd been to my office dozens of times. She had been to all the employee events since she was a child. She was worried about our finances. She offered to quit school and come home if it would help. That really got to me."

## Friendship's Glow

"Trust me, you find out who your real friends
and colleagues are at pivotal points in your life
and career—one of which is when you're seeking

employment-related assistance, and the other is when
you need help moving a couch out of the basement."

— RANDY

Lost relationships due to fear or betrayal or self-preservation were common throughout the stories of those I talked with. Yet many of them also described numerous acts of kindness and support from other friends and coworkers. Occasionally these acts marked the beginning of a deeper friendship.

On a Friday afternoon, Brenda was let go with no notice. She left the office and was told she could come in Saturday with human resources to clear out her personal items. "The next day one of my employees showed up to help me pack. I told her she could go. I was afraid for her. They could fire her over this. She said she knew that, but she was going to be here anyway. Ultimately she and I are tighter now. We are lifelong friends. We are friends—way beyond work. It took a lot of courage for her to do it."

Diane had many friends over the twenty-eight years at her organization, but not all of them reached out. "The people that did reach out… it was funny. The very strong Christians reached out."

Lori recalled that despite being told by their employer not to contact her, "A couple of them did, despite the gag order, and we are still friends. One just retired and the other told them off and left. They couldn't stand to work there after that. They thought it was unfair. The husband of one of them was in facilities management, and he was the one who cleaned out my office. I felt better that a friend was cleaning it out."

"The friends you thought you had and the ones you end up having—that was an amazing thing," Nick recalled. "The day I walked out, no one was there. The next day I walked out with two cardboard boxes. It was the holiday. My assistant came and asked if I was ready to go. The parking garage was far away. She locked arms with me and said, 'Let's go, friend.' I walked into a sterile parking garage and drove home. I thought, '*That* is a friend.'"

"I got a note from a colleague," Bruce remembered, "saying he would help me look for a new job and that he missed my leadership. It's always nice to hear that. Several people wrote me letters of recommendations.

I appreciated the recommendations. Greg, another colleague, calls me once a month. And another colleague called and said, 'I am so sorry.' She said she could relate, having worked for the same person that I did at one time.

Don described to me how his coworkers assembled in the parking lot while he was being escorted out, "As I walked out to the parking lot, I had a chance to say goodbye to our team. Some cried, many used the word *railroaded.* I hugged them and shook their hands with the security guard in tow. I loaded up my car and drove to the gate. Without a card I couldn't open the gate to leave; cars stacked up behind me. My manager went into the guard booth and told them something. The guards, who knew the actual hours I worked, were so shocked they couldn't open the gate for a few moments."

Like Don, Mona mentioned friends who rose to the occasion. "One friend took me to lunch. We were talking, and I said I didn't have a car—my company car had been taken back when I lost my job. He immediately offered to lend me one of his family's cars for the summer. His son was going to be away, and his car would be available if I needed it. I was so touched by his generosity. What a nice thing to do. You can't get a car loan without a job. And you can't drive to a job interview without a car. Another friend reached out to me and told me her story. She was let go from her company a year ago. Now employed, she offered to introduce me to her boss who might be able to offer me some consulting opportunities while I am looking for a full-time job—another incredible gesture. And I did meet her boss, and she did hire me to do some part-time consulting."

## Conan and Garry

The people I talked with described many acts of kindness from friends who really rose to the occasion when they were most needed. I conclude this chapter with Conan O'Brien's description of the special kind of friend Garry Shandling was to him when he was fired from *The Tonight Show*. The evening of comedian Garry Shandling's death, Conan O'Brien paid tribute to him on TBS, not as a comedian, but as a friend. Conan said that for him the loss was great because of what Gary meant to him personally.

"I have to tell you this is a devastating shock to me and just about everyone I know. This doesn't seem real." He went on to say that for the next several days others would talk about Garry's comic mastery. "I am thinking about Garry Shandling the person. He was also sensitive, complicated, and he had a ton of empathy for other people. He really did care.

During a particularly difficult time in my life, as fate would have it, Garry just magically appeared and he helped me a lot... I think it's seven years ago when my *Tonight Show* ended in this crazy, spectacular, effed-up fashion. I woke up the next morning and I had no job, and I had no idea what I was going to do. I was shell-shocked. I was a complete zombie." His wife suggested a week in Hawaii. "My wife took our two kids to the beach. 'Let's leave Daddy alone.' I just sat alone in this hotel room for half an hour, forty minutes, just silent, not knowing what to do. And I could hear the ocean—I'm just sitting there—and suddenly the phone rang. It was Garry Shandling, who was staying in the same hotel.

This was a week I was supposed to spend with my wife and kids. I spent the entire week with Garry Shandling. I was at a real low point. He counseled me, he cheered me up, and he told me jokes. He talked to me about philosophy. He talked to me about how there are bigger things in the world and how I was going to be fine. He talked about Eckhart Tolle—about all this amazing stuff. We had an incredible one afternoon; I think the last afternoon that we spent together on that island. We took this really long walk. We climbed over lava formations, we went through a cave, we went to this far part of the island, and we saw a little stretch of sand, and we laid down on it. And the sun started to go down. And we're both watching the sun go down, and I turned to Garry and I said, "Garry, this is the most romantic moment of my life, and it's with you." He was an incredibly generous person.

## Key Takeaways

1. Be cautious about workplace friendships, especially with bosses or human resources. Think carefully about whom to trust and confide in.
2. Be aware that if you are let go, your former coworkers may be afraid to associate with you for fear they may lose their jobs.
3. Remember your priorities. Focus time and effort on your relationships with family and friends.
4. If you know someone who has been fired, be there for him or her.

# CHAPTER 9

## BURN UNIT RECOVERY: COPING WITH SUDDEN JOB LOSS

> "You can't eat eight hours a day nor drink
> for eight hours a day nor make love for eight
> hours—all you can do for eight hours is work.
> Which is the reason why man makes himself and
> everybody else so miserable and unhappy."
> —WILLIAM FAULKNER

My father was fired from his job. At fifty-five he was let go from his position in finance for a manufacturer. He was devastated, and as the sole breadwinner, very concerned about how he would support his family. Although it was more than thirty years ago, I have a vivid picture of him during the days immediately after he lost his job. In the morning I would find him on the couch, sitting up straight on the middle cushion, dressed in a gray three-piece suit and tie, and his shoes were shined. His hands were at his side. He looked ready to go to work but just sat and stared directly ahead. I asked him why he was all dressed up. He'd had the same routine his entire adult life—getting up, showering, shaving, getting dressed, putting on his tie, having his coffee and breakfast, and driving off to work. Suddenly without a job, he didn't know what else to do, so he kept his same routine.

Eventually he began his job search. This was before the Internet, e-mail, and computers. He had our dining room table covered with the want ads from the newspapers. He sat with a typewriter, envelopes, and stamps and sent out résumés in the mail every day. He would eagerly go to the mailbox, only to find rejection letters. After nearly ten months, he found work.

To be suddenly unemployed is challenging to those like my dad who are used to getting up and going to work each day. Between getting ready for, commuting to, and actually doing the work, there are easily fifty to sixty hours a week devoted to full-time work. That doesn't include the time people might spend traveling for work, attending events, or even working beyond a forty-hour workweek. Aside from spending extensive time looking for work, how do people who were once busy with full-time jobs spend their newfound yet unwanted spare time? How do they fill the void?

Related to this, how do people cope with being suddenly unemployed? How do they manage their new financial circumstances as well as the emotional impact of being let go?

## Recovery after Surgery

> "I put off surgery for years because
> I was a loyal employee."
> —MARK

After being let go, three of the interviewees spent their time recovering from surgery. Recall that Connie was given notice from her law firm while undergoing outpatient therapy after her knee replacement. She spent the time immediately after her dismissal continuing to recover and rehabilitate. Mark had surgery, one he had put off for seven years, after being let go.

Diane was scheduled for breast surgery on the Tuesday after she her job was eliminated. For weeks following her termination, she was in great pain, recovering at home from the surgery. The operation went badly; the surgeon nicked some nerves. The physical pain was so intense she was unable to do much of anything, including worrying about or grieving her job loss.

## Family Ties

> "My parents both needed more of my help. They lived
> nearby, so I could help them out more, take them to
> appointments, bring them meals, visit with them."
> —PAIGE

Most of the people in this study used some of their newfound free time to spend with family and friends. Elizabeth discovered that her husband enjoyed having her home. "I visited my mom a bit more. I became my husband's secretary. He loved having a housewife. He didn't want me to go back to work." After working full time her entire married life, Melissa shared that she was finally able to spend time with her family. "I participated in my son's life to a great extent, so that got us closer."

Nick too talked about the opportunity he had to spend more time with his daughter, who was a senior in high school when Nick lost his job. "My daughter would get up and have breakfast with me. At ten we'd watch the TV show *Lost* together. She went to school, and I went back to work on my job search. We spent tons of time together, and it was great. We made the most out of it."

Gail was let go the day she returned from maternity leave. Her time was consumed fairly quickly with the new baby. Gail was able to be a full-time parent for the first year of her child's life.

For some of the interviewees, spending more time with family meant caring for an elderly parent. Bruce described how he used the opportunity to see his family. "A year ago, my mother moved, so I have been able to go with her to doctors, oncologists. She had cancer surgery, and I was there for her; I went through that with her. She's not that good with doctors. I was the go-between with my siblings. Family has consumed me. I read more. I try to not watch TV during the day."

Julie too found herself in the caregiver role when she became unemployed. "I had to take Mom to the hospital. We ended up finding out that my mom was diagnosed with stage-three cancer. For the next ten months, I sat with my mom and daughter and laughed, cried, fought, and drove. It was medicine for all three of us. Ten months were mine with her. I got to share them with her. After those ten months, I was her caregiver."

Similarly, Connie experienced that with her new free time she could take care of her mother and become her primary caregiver. "I had more time for my family. My mom was getting older and needed a lot of help. I had more time for her."

When Paige recognized she would be unable to meet her supervisor's expectations, she negotiated her own departure. "My parents both needed more of my help. They lived nearby, so I could help them out more, take them to appointments, bring them meals, visit with them. They died a few months after I was let go, so it was good that I got to see them as much as I did."

Some people took advantage of the time to spend it with their family members. Becoming a family caregiver was the new role several of the participants took on after losing their job.

## Interests

"I found that gyms aren't as crowded during the day."
—WES

Several people filled the void with a range of other activities. Elizabeth used her time to volunteer at her church's food pantry. Lori was in the middle of her doctoral program when she was let go, so she spent her time focusing on her dissertation. Mark filled his days with things he used to enjoy, such as music. "I love it. I try to play the piano every day. I decided to get back into cooking. I experimented with spices, sauces. I was on a roll, cooking for my wife when she walked in the door. Piddling, fixing things that I might not have done otherwise. I worked in my garden constantly—my herbs, my perennials. I had to do those things." Melissa also found time for things she enjoyed. "I read more, watched more TV. I walked all the time, trying to get my thoughts going, and kept remembering, 'Seek and ye shall find.'"

Lack of funds got in the way of Sondra's activities. She admitted she initially spent her days on the couch watching TV. "Shopping or going out to lunch is expensive. The things I like to do cost money. For not working, I would never use myself as an example. I was so hard on myself. I was so stressed out. I found workout videos on YouTube—that didn't cost money. It was hard to find the motivation to exercise though."

"I ate. I gained a lot of weight. I ate my feelings. Later in therapy I learned it was emotional eating," Julie confessed.

Some of the people interviewed enjoyed their leisure time. Paige took advantage of the opportunity to relax. "It was summer, so I spent a lot of time at the pool with a drink. It was relaxing, and I spent some time with my best friend." Bruce shared, "I have to tell you, it's nice not working. I've been unemployed seven months. I may retire, I don't know. I love talking to people about things besides work. Work is boring conversation. There is so much more in life. I may write a book."

Noting that it's important to stay busy, Wes warned, "Avoid hanging out at home and feeling sorry for yourself, although that happens too."

It may be a surprising finding, but for some, the void of not working was filled by travel. Wes said the first thing he did was go to Hawaii with his family. His firing did not interrupt their planned vacation. In addition to caring for her mother, Connie did a lot of traveling. "I went on a cruise with a friend, went to my law school reunion, and went to Vegas with a friend." Looking on the bright side, Connie had a new realization that she didn't have to fit things in around her work schedule. "Wow, I can go whenever I want. I don't have to worry about work. Wow, I don't have to go to Costco on Saturday. I can go any day."

Travel provided a healing experience for Brenda. She had always wanted to go to Africa. After being fired, she and her sister, who she was not close to, traveled there together. "We refer to this all the time—we didn't know each other. I lost my job. She had a personal crisis. We flew to Africa for three weeks. By the third week we became good friends. We came back to that many times. It was an incredibly healing time. Her husband left her in a year. Who was her support? It was me. She considers me her best friend. A life-changing event—Africa is a healing place. The world is so much bigger than my little problems. That was my healing."

It may seem odd that people travel and enjoy themselves after losing a job, but it might be a good step toward healing writes Rebecca Knight in her article "How to Bounce Back After Getting Laid Off" on the Harvard Business Review website. "In the immediate aftermath of a job loss, give yourself time to decompress by 'taking a vacation of sorts,' suggests Priscilla Claman, the president of Career Strategies, a Boston-based consulting firm, and a contributor to the *HBR Guide to Getting the Right Job.* 'You don't need to go to Aruba, but take a break,' even if it's just for a weekend or a few days, she says. Your goal is get out of your own head with a fun and 'active hiatus.' Go hiking. Go camping. Go kayaking. 'The first phase is recovery,' says John Lees, the UK-based career strategist and the author of *How to Get a Job You Love.* Don't make any big decisions in those first few days and don't rush into the job market the day after you've received the news. You need time to process what happened and 'how you feel about it.'"

## Coping

Job loss has financial, emotional, and even spiritual repercussions. The people I interviewed engaged a variety of strategies to cope with job loss.

## Managing Financial Challenges

> "I didn't have money to do manicures. I did
> have WIC and food stamps, so I ate."
> —JULIE

Cutting back on expenses was a common and expected strategy. Bruce remarked, "I do things we used to pay for. I clean, I cook. We don't go out nearly as much. I painted the deck." Likewise, Elizabeth and her husband cut back. "One thing that helped us get through this is my husband and I adjusted our spending habits and adapted accordingly so we could maintain a lifestyle that we were used to." Elizabeth told me that her husband wanted me to know that.

Mark shared his cost-cutting activities. "My survivalist instincts clicked in right away. I looked at everything and looked at what expenses I could get rid of. We made a commitment to stop eating out. We live off her salary, and mine is for the unforeseen expenses. And it has helped. It's been great. We are more frugal and careful, but we don't deprive ourselves. We still do what we like."

Along with her family, Melissa cut costs and saved money by finding free activities. "We had to drastically cut expenses. I immediately went on unemployment. It isn't much. Our family found lots of free things to do like museums, parks, and festivals."

One of the most dramatic cost-cutting activities was selling a house. Randy put his house on the market in anticipation of not being able to find work in the area. He and his wife sold their house and into an apartment to reduce expenses. He realized it might be difficult to get a job at his former pay level. Randy also thought moving back to his hometown where he knew more people would make it easier to find work.

In addition to cutting costs, the interviewees found different ways to add to their incomes. Connie said, "I withdrew my money from my retirement account, and we survived. I lived on deferred compensation for a year to pay for my bills. Make sure you have savings. I took unemployment, and it was a little spending money. Why not?"

As for unemployment payments, Mark recalled, "You have to jump through a lot of hoops. I couldn't get any. I've never been without a job. I never had unemployment. They looked at me like I was trying to scam them."

Julie said, "I went straight to the Medicaid office and filed for benefits and then filed for unemployment the morning after I left. We also filed for bankruptcy. I was the family breadwinner. My husband worked part time. We had to spend down my entire 401(k) to keep our house. I had just bought a van, and we had to turn it back in. It was rough; it caused a lot of stress on our marriage. I had to be the one to fix it."

Joe's wife, Sharon, claimed that while Joe was out of work for two years, "We went through all our savings. Everything we had. We had to take out a loan. We are still paying it off."

For some, job loss meant cutting back on expenses, taking uncomfortable but not unreasonable steps. Several were a part of two-income households so could rely on the other person's income. But for others, losing a job had dramatic financial consequences. Some acquired new debt through loans or credit cards. Many spent down or depleted their savings, including their retirement funds. One person sold his home and moved to prepare for a lower cost lifestyle. One family filed for bankruptcy.

## Family and Friends

Individuals leaned on their families and friends emotional support. Lori explained, "I coped by surrounding myself with my kids and their activities. It hit them hard. One was in high school and one was in junior high. I kept busy with family. They said I had their total support. The logic was that I was unemployed. They made it seem OK. Even my fellow students were supportive; it helped me see the bigger picture. That opened up a lot of possibilities. It wasn't just volunteering; it was bringing people together at a high level. The potential was there in the ability to change and make a difference."

Melissa also found support from her family. "I coped with help from family and friends. We got to travel and have fun together. The best coping is to stay busy. You are going from a train going 150 miles an hour to watching *Jeopardy*. That doesn't get your brainpower going. Take a few weeks off and then get busy."

Sondra, twenty-two, was living on her own when she was fired and lived far away from her parents. She relied on her extended family who lived in the area. "My relatives helped me. And you hate to ask family for money or for loans. They checked in on me, took me out to lunch. I would go over to my grandparents for the day. Sitting home alone, I could only think about being unemployed. They helped me take my mind off it."

Connie found support from a friend who had been through a similar experience. "I saw a good friend also get fired—there were others. That helps. Misery loves company."

## Spiritual

> "I know it was God who got me through it."
> —DIANE

Faith played a major role in coping with job loss for several of those interviewed. Elizabeth sought out her church family for support after she was let go. Often interviewees would make remarks like Connie's, "I keep thinking, things happen for a reason. You just have to stay positive." Others would invoke blessings through prayer or worship.

Compounding the emotional pain following Diane's job loss, her breast surgery resulted in her having to endure intense physical pain. "I know it was God who got me through it," she recalled emotionally. "It was prayer and family. People reached out to me and were supportive. That made a difference. I prayed a lot." Diane said she sought comfort from this Bible verse in Jeremiah 29:11: "I know the plans I have for you."

After being fired for the third time, Brenda she went home dejected and asked, "All right, God, what do You want me to do? I surrender. I will do whatever *You* want. And I just sat…I am going to watch TV and do what I always said I would do: turn it over to God. I never really do; this time I'm turning it over to God. I'm going to be quiet, really quiet. I am going to listen. Maybe the answer will come. Three days later my phone rang. An organization asked me to look at a position. They just wanted *me*; I didn't have to interview. Two days later I got another offer. And that is where I am now. Two positions, same salary. Both of them said the job was mine if I wanted it. I have been here fourteen years."

Faith was a key part of coping for Lori. A devoutly religious person, she said simply, "God had plans for you, everything your spirit needs to hear, although you doubt it. That speaks to the need in my spirit."

For Nick, coping meant not focusing on what had happened, but rather on creating his next great opportunity. "In a way you could say I got screwed, but I bounced instead. If you hit with a thud, you get demoralized. But you are going to get exactly what you are putting out. If you bounce, it starts to seem better. You apply places; you talk to people in your network. All of a sudden you see what could come of this. It's been far from perfect. Coping for me was not thinking something bad happened, that there was a breakdown. I wasn't going to let that be my story. I bounced."

Adamantly, Diane asserted, "I was determined not to let this define me."

## Forgiveness and Coming to Terms

> "I stopped hating. It made a huge difference. I hung a
> picture from my old job proudly. I am beyond all of it."
> —NICK

Coming to terms with a job loss isn't easy. Coming to terms with it or ultimately forgiving those who fired them was a key coping strategy for a few of those interviewed. Gail sought help to get through her job loss. "I had a coach who was very good about helping me see the dynamics, the triangulation, and see that it wasn't me. And he reminded me of that often. Sometimes things happen when you don't take care of it yourself. Because I had been done with the job for a year before I left, I think I had processed it already. When it happened, I had already processed a lot."

Forgiveness was integral to Diane's own healing. "I had to forgive them, or I would be very bitter. I realized I did what I did for the people I served. They couldn't take that from me. I had done what I had done out of love." Like Diane, Nick saw the value in coming to terms with the people who fired him. "The other thing I had to do was to stop hating the people who did this to me. I didn't want a voodoo doll. I just wanted to realize it happened and move on. To this day my wife would love to stick pins in the person who fired me. It's been hard for me. I sold twenty-three logo items for next to nothing at a garage sale."

## Key Takeaways

1. Losing a job has financial, emotional, and even spiritual repercussions. As many experts suggest, save enough money to last you up to six months. It's difficult enough finding a job, let alone

trying to appear confident and poised, when you are worried about how to pay your bills.

2.  Get a line of credit while you are employed. You may never need it, but you won't be able to get one if you are unemployed.

3.  If your job loss is sudden, take a few days to adjust. Try not to discuss your situation with others outside your inner circle.

4.  Take care of yourself as much as possible. Maintain positive re-lationships with your family and friends and stay involved with nonwork activities. If you lose your job, you will need a support system and new ways to spend your time.

5.  Recovery from job loss is a process and a journey. Discover the methods of coping that appeal to you.

6.  Finding a job is a full-time job in itself. If you are let go, take a few days to absorb the shock, and then get busy looking for work.

# PART 3

## ADVICE FROM THE FIRING LINE

"My best advice is always be prepared that the next day is your last day at work."

"Now I know you have to look out for yourself."

# CHAPTER 10

## FIRE PREVENTION EDUCATION: ADVICE FOR THOSE STILL EMPLOYED

This book is meant to be helpful to those who are currently employed, not just those who have lost their jobs. Just as you buy insurance in case of an accident, the time to prepare for job loss is when you have a job. The people interviewed for this book offer a wealth of advice for those who are employed. Many of them expressed that they wished they knew then what they know now.

The bottom line is this: It's best to be prepared for unexpected job loss, even if you don't suspect it. Take advantage of the interviewees' advice and learn from their experiences.

### Keep Looking

> "Headhunters, recruiters, called frequently. I wish I had taken the time to meet with them when they called."
> —NICK

Over and over, my interviewees described themselves as loyal and engaged employees. Most of them had more than five years with their company. It may surprise you that most of them recommend keeping an eye out for and evaluating new opportunities even if you are happily employed.

Most of the participants in this study had not done this. They were either too busy to take the time, too loyal to their employers, or felt happy and secure with their current situations. Surprised at their terminations, they wished they had paid attention to the external job market while they were still employed.

Summing it up, Nick shares, "I never even looked anywhere else. I had worked there for fifteen years. I was happy and had had a lot of career progression. So I never looked. And there were lots of opportunities. Headhunters, recruiters, called frequently. I wish I had taken the time to meet with them when they called."

Just taking the time to learn about new opportunities is a challenge, according to Janice. She recommended keeping an open mind: "I would advise people who are working to talk to headhunters. I didn't talk to recruiters or contacts. I was too busy, and I liked what I did."

Similarly, Melissa recalled, "I didn't talk to recruiters. We were such a good team; I thought no one would break it up. It was going so well." Melissa's loyalty to the team as well as her belief that she was a valuable contributor kept her from looking elsewhere.

Wes was fired due to some changes in upper management. "I had a boss I didn't like, and if you don't want to play politics, maybe it's time to start searching on your own. Looking back, I should have started the search on my own." He admitted that while he was caught in the crossfire between two players in upper management, *he thought his individual performance and integrity would keep him safe.* Being on the wrong side, Wes was fired unceremoniously.

These individuals and others thought loyalty was a two-way street. They didn't recognize that their loyalty and tenure might not be rewarded. As such, they ignored headhunter calls, neglected to seek out other opportunities, and never imagined themselves leaving their employment.

## Keep Your Résumé Updated with Accomplishments

If you are happy in your job and are not looking for other opportunities, it is likely you don't have an updated résumé. The people I interviewed strongly encourage you to maintain your résumé and have it available on your *home* computer or a flash drive.

Most job postings require sending a current résumé as part of your application. When you are employed, maintaining a current résumé is often not a priority. Most of the people I talked with didn't anticipate the need for an updated résumé.

"No job is permanent. I had a boss who said, 'Never let the ink on your résumé get dry,'" cautioned Randy, who worked out a departure from his employer after three years in management.

It is generally believed that the best résumés showcase the individual's accomplishments, preferably with metrics. Here is a key point to remember: Those accomplishments and related metrics are more difficult to acquire if you are no longer with the company. You will likely not have access to the data you need to demonstrate your effectiveness. For example, you may know that you increased sales in your last position, and that is a strong achievement. But that achievement is made stronger if you can say you increased sales by X percent or had a 95 percent customer rating. You may have lowered employee turnover, increased membership, improved cash flow, or increased ROI, but without the company data, it's difficult to say by how much.

Karen described what she practiced: "I kept notes on my accomplishments on my iPad at home. I had been let go once, and I had to scramble to look for facts to support my accomplishments. So now I keep a running list of my duties and success factors at home in case I need to update my résumé in a hurry. That said, it would have been better to have updated my résumé as well, but at least I had the facts."

Another way to keep a list of your accomplishments is to update your LinkedIn profile, which serves as a digital résumé. Again, it's important to assemble and quantify your achievements while you are employed.

In addition, there is a psychological reason for having your résumé current and ready to go. Losing a job is deflating and depressing. In chapter 8, the interviewees shared their emotional reactions to losing their jobs: devastation, depression, anger, and loss of self-esteem. These emotions take their toll, making it very difficult to summon the energy and the confidence needed to put together a document that tells people why they should hire you. Having a résumé ready to go and reviewing your accomplishments can give you a boost and makes it much easier to start applying for jobs.

And importantly, keep a copy of your résumé on a flash drive or personal computer at home. Having it at work won't help if you get fired and are ushered out of the building immediately.

## Keep Your Personal and Professional Contact Information at Home

> "People were calling and e-mailing my work phone and
> e-mail, so I missed many of their calls and e-mails."
> —MONA

As you leave your job, you will have to turn over your work cell phone, computer, and other work-related equipment. You will no longer have access to any of your contact information stored on those devices.

As Mona explained, "I always just had one phone, the one work provided. I didn't want to have to carry around two phones, so I just used my work cell phone. When I was fired, my company cell phone and laptop were taken immediately. They wouldn't let me access any information on them. I had no way to reach my contacts or for them to reach me. People were calling and e-mailing my work phone and e-mail, so I missed many of their calls and e-mails."

The experience of leaving for Janice was distressing, "I had some personal things on my work laptop. Nothing bad, just some files for my parents and photos of my grandchildren. I traveled all the time, and it wasn't feasible to carry two laptops. So before I left, the company let one of my coworkers see my files. They said they didn't, but someone in Information Services told me they did. I wasn't able to get those files back." Janice lost photos and the documents related to her parents' affairs. Given that most companies have a policy against using work equipment for personal business, and given that the information on a work device belongs to the company, use caution when deciding what to store on company equipment. Use a flash drive (although many companies do not allow a flash drive) or the Google Drive to store personal documents, passwords, and photos so you always have access to them.

More ominous warnings come from Melissa, "Remember that your phones and e-mails are monitored. Don't do anything on your work computer or phone that you wouldn't want on the front page of the newspaper. Some companies will turn on the GPS tracking in your phone to ensure you are where you're supposed to be."

If you have lost a job, you will need to be able to reach out to your contacts. It is critical to keep contact information at home. With LinkedIn and professional associations, it is often possible to search out contact information. But remember, if you are without a job, you will not feel like rebuilding your contact list. With your own e-mail and phone lists, you will be able to disseminate your own exit story and announce your plans. (More on that later.)

Keep minimal personal items at work. If you are let go, you may be allowed to come back on the weekend or in the evening to remove your personal items. However, some companies have an employee clean out your desk for you. This means someone is going through your things, which adds salt to the wound. Do not keep anything at work that you wouldn't want your company knowing about.

## Maintain a Professional LinkedIn Presence

Another way to preserve and grow your contacts is by maintaining a strong LinkedIn presence. Again, it is easier to build your network while you have a job. LinkedIn has become a key platform for networking and recruiting. Having a compelling LinkedIn profile is almost as important as having a good résumé. You will want to build this while you are employed. It will enable you to attract and gain a greater number of contacts. In addition, LinkedIn provides an excellent means to develop your professional brand and be seen as a resource or expert in your field. Recruiters use LinkedIn extensively.

Randy commented on the usefulness of LinkedIn: "Before LinkedIn you used to have to go to task forces and meetings in your industry. I have linked in a lot and reconnected with lots of people."

A professional profile means a professional photo as well. Do not post a photo of you and your family, your latest vacation, or you in your jeans and a T-shirt unless the type of job you want relates to these things. Get a professional photo of you dressed for the job you want.

## Know Your Employer's Social Media Policy

Your company's social media policy, while often unevenly enforced, could be a reason used to fire someone. Social media expert Jill Rowley was let go from her job for violating her company's media policy. "To them it's black and white that I spoke with a reporter from *Ad Age*. And the reality is if you Google 'Jill Rowley' or just go to my LinkedIn profile, you will see that I've spoken to lots of bloggers, lots of thought leaders, lots of experts in the community telling them exactly what I told the *Ad Age* reporter. But the fact that the *Ad Age* guy was a quote reporter, I violated the policy."

And it should go without saying that your Facebook page should be free of controversial posts and photos. Employers and potential employers will check Facebook.

## Know Your Employer's Policy on Vacation and Sick Time

> "It makes me sick that I lost nine
> hundred hours of sick time."
> — CONNIE

As a general rule, it is good to use your vacation time to take a break—so you come back to work refreshed. There is another reason to take your vacation. Employers do not necessarily have to pay your accrued vacation if they fire you. It depends on the state and the employer's policies. You need to know these policies so you can plan accordingly.

The impact of Melissa's termination was made worse when her employer would not pay out accrued, unused vacation time. "I was unable to take my vacation because we were always working. We'd lost a couple of key players, and the rest of us had to pitch in. But when they fired me, they would not give me my vacation. Here I didn't take vacation because I was loyal to them and because they needed me, and then when they no longer needed me, they wouldn't pay me for my unused vacation time. So, I tell people to take their vacations.

"I went to my lawyer, and she told me managers had no protection. There wasn't much communication. She wouldn't help me negotiate because she said they had all the cards. Maybe I should have gone to a different lawyer, I don't know. I wrote back to the human resources director to ask him to pay my vacation, and he quoted the employee handbook."

Others caution that taking time off can be risky. It is easier to make plans to fire someone when he or she is not in the office. Having someone away at a conference or on vacation is the perfect way for the company to discuss the termination, get the legal, security, and HR departments' buy-in, and plan who, when, where, and how the termination is going to occur.

The same goes for using sick time. After twenty-eight years with a law firm, Connie had banked a great deal of sick time. Being a solid employee, she did not call in sick simply to take time off work. She had an outstanding attendance record. "Not everyone who got fired was lucky like me. I could draw on my retirement. It makes me sick that I lost nine hundred hours of sick time."

Recall that some people, like Mark, put off surgeries, medical procedures, and other health-care needs because they are too busy with work. Being a loyal employee, not thinking of your own needs, can be detrimental to your health.

Melissa strongly recommends doing the opposite: "First, for your health's sake, don't put it off. Have your surgeries, procedures, and even checkups now, while you are employed." Second, she explained that people should take care of themselves while they have employer-subsidized insurance and paid sick leave or disability. While you may be able to purchase COBRA to continue your health-care coverage for eighteen months following your job departure, health insurance doesn't cover all the costs. While you are employed, there is greater likelihood of being able to afford the copayments and deductibles. When you're unemployed, it becomes more difficult to meet everyday living expenses, let alone cover any expensive medical care."

While unemployed you have more time to undergo medical procedures and recover from them. However, the downside is you need energy and health to mount a job search. Having medical procedures and surgeries may require a recovery period. And as with Mark and Diane, some surgeries and procedures cause a great deal of pain. All this delays and impairs your ability to look for a job. It's important to have key medical procedures and surgeries done while you're employed.

Benefits, like paid vacation and sick days, and health insurance are part of an employee's compensation. Many companies have the "use it or lose it" approach. It's important to know your employer's policy so you do not lose valuable benefits.

## Understand Your Employer's Termination Policies and Practices

Gail encourages employees to "really understand the HR policies and severance policies, and ask related questions. Find out how people get fired in the organization. What is the culture of being fired?" Lee learned quickly about his new company's culture on his first day when he was told to pick out a desk. As he sat down at one of them, a nearby coworker said, "Don't sit there. Anyone who sits there gets fired." Gail suggests talking directly with human resources and reading the reports on Glassdoor, a job-search website that also reviews companies. If you are interviewing for a position, ask what happened to the person who held it last.

## Be Involved in Activities Outside of Your Professional Field

Career-oriented people often use their spare time to engage in work-related activities like reading industry journals, attending seminars, and participating in professional associations. Those interviewed strongly encourage you to be active in *non-work-related* activities as well. Here are their three biggest reasons: First, if you lose your job, you need something to keep you connected and engaged with others. Often professional activities are discontinued when you are terminated. While you can maintain memberships in professional associations, it is difficult to continue participation in trade associations without being employed. But community, faith-based, sports, or hobby-related activities are not attached to your role as a professional. These you can continue beyond your professional world.

Second, a job loss often includes a loss of social connections and networks. Fellow participants in your community activities can provide you with much-needed support and networking opportunities. Third, and possibly most important, these activities, along with your friends and family, remind you that *you are not your job*. You can find enjoyment, meaning, and purpose outside the workplace.

A warning comes with this advice as well. Some employers want your total dedication and availability. Some companies reward people who make personal sacrifices and offer their complete dedication. In general, it may be best not to discuss your social activities with coworkers.

## Build Bridges within Your Industry

While you are working is the best time to build relationships with people in your industry, including your vendors and competitors. It is hard but advisable to get away from work on occasion to attend meetings, cocktail parties, or dinners, or to serve on industry-specific task forces. The next time you go to a meeting, trade show, conference, or task force, look around. Check out the hotel bars. When you go out to eat, observe who is together. These people are often networking—fishing for their next jobs or creating their own safety nets. Consider doing the same.

To underscore this point, Randy advised, "I would recommend networking a whole lot more, whether or not you know a change is coming. It's a bitch to build a network and reconnect when suddenly you need to. Act as if you don't have a job and build your network on an ongoing basis. External networking is done the whole time. But it becomes more active when you are let go. No job is permanent. You should start building bridges as soon as you hit the job market."

## Cultivate Good Working Relationships with Your Coworkers

Cultivating relationships is easier said than done, but it's essential. It's a small world, and people will show up when you least expect them. Bill was fired from a finance position. He applied for a similar position at a company in another state. At a trade association dinner, the hiring manager at that company met one of Bill's former employees, who now worked in that state. As they talked, the hiring manager learned of their connection and asked the former employee what he thought of Bill. The former colleague had a challenging time working with Bill and didn't want to recommend him to a colleague. He knew not to disparage him, so he simply said, "He's a nice guy." Whether that lack of endorsement was instrumental or not, Bill did not get the job. If Bill had cultivated a better relationship with his employee, he might have gotten an endorsement and the job.

Having a good relationship with colleagues can also provide you with reinforcements to your safety net. If you are on good terms, they may assist you in your job search. Coworkers who move to a new company will likely hear about new job openings. As said earlier, having someone on the inside vouch for you is a tremendous advantage in a job search.

## Keep a File

> *"You will find a time in your career when*
> *you have to defend yourself."*
> —LORI

Several of the people interviewed commented on the importance of keeping your own documentation of important directions, feedback, or events. Diane was let go shortly after she got a new boss. At first she had a positive relationship with him. The relationship deteriorated as her boss made unfounded accusations about her. Diane kept notes. "I kept a file called 'unpleasant topics,' which I forwarded home along with any of his communications. Great documentation of everything in case I had to sue."

Lori too encourages people to take notes. "I would tell people not to be paranoid but to keep good records of what's said and done. Use your chain of command, and keep a paper trail so you can defend yourself. You will find a time in your career when you have to defend yourself. I guess it's your way of showing that you did communicate, to show you did your due diligence so false accusations don't stick. You have to be a little more suspicious of people's motives and intentions. That's what blindsided me. I couldn't believe someone would look at me and make judgments and lie. I couldn't believe people would do that." Again, keep your files at home.

## Ask for Feedback, Do Your Research

Sometimes we are not aware when there is a problem or if someone is unhappy with our work. Randy reflected on his time with a company where he wasn't a good fit and what he would have done differently. "Probably I would have forced feedback more often from my boss. I wouldn't wait for others to share it—they won't. If it were me again, I would force myself onto more leaders, asking them for feedback on my department, on me, to build my knowledge base faster. You have to be able to read between the lines. A lot of people only look at their own job and keep their head down. I was stepping in it the whole time. If you force the issue, you have more crucial conversations in managing your own career."

Mark regretted leaving a good job and moving to another one, where he was fired after one year. "The grass is not always greener. I did a lot of research before I jumped. Once you tender a resignation, you are done with that company. You have to weigh it out. I did that. I had a litany of questions. Prepare yourself. Ask the right questions of the new company you are going to. Look at mission, strategy, bottom line." He warned against the promises some companies make to lure you into accepting an employment offer, especially when they say that in a year you'll be at "this level." "Alarm bells should go off. It's a compromise they aren't prepared to do."

## Appreciate Your Job, Do It Well, but Don't Let Your Job Own You

"Whatever you do, do a good job at it."
—JANICE

Even after being let go from their jobs, those interviewed maintained a strong work ethic. They advise everyone with a job to work hard, but also to maintain work-life balance. Nick advises those with jobs "to appreciate the opportunity you have been given. Be sincere, act with integrity." Likewise, Joe said he takes "every opportunity to not take anything for granted. You can be doing the best job and be successful, but for reasons beyond your control, you can lose your job."

"Whatever you do, do a good job at it. People see that you care, and you have a good feeling about what you are doing, so you are able to give more," Janice recommends.

"Well, I am a person who is driven. I say, say yes to things," Lesley commented. "I would never be where I am if I didn't work my ass off. I would do anything. If nothing else, it gives you clout. They knew I understood because I worked in all areas so I could learn and understand. I did clerical stuff to learn. It helps as a leader if you can show you will work. Make yourself indispensable."

"Do your job" is Elizabeth's message as well. But she adds, "Just do your job and leave it there." Elizabeth also warns that sometimes "the boss wants someone to work all night. When I leave at five o'clock, they want me to do more. They think I don't have enough work if I can finish and go home at five o'clock when it's time to go. I've worked all day, and it's time to go."

## Friday, 4:00 p.m., No Subject Line

An unexpected meeting request without a subject line to indicate the purpose of the meeting is often a sign of impending termination. Mona recalled, "I received an e-mail invitation to a meeting with no subject. I wrote to my manager's assistant and asked her what it was. She knew, but she lied and said she had no idea. The meeting was set up to tell me I was being let go."

The timing of the termination is vital. Melissa explained, "Never take a meeting in the last week of the month that seems strange or out of place. Please, you need health insurance. Don't come in to work when people can get ahold of you." Health insurance generally provides coverage for the calendar month. When someone is let go, it discontinues the last day of that month. It's actually better to be fired the first week of the month so your employer-provided health insurance lasts longer."

Melissa went even further: "Make sure if you are scheduled for a strange meeting that you call in sick so you can use your paid time off. I never took a sick day. That doesn't count for anything except your own integrity. My integrity didn't pay the bills. It's sad to say, but true. If I knew then what I know now, I would not only *not* come in on the thirtieth, I would have continued to call in sick for several days to get my act together. You don't want to be surprised because you have to leave immediately. What are you going to say? You aren't prepared for that."

Melissa sums it up with some strong words of advice: "My best advice is always be prepared that the next day is your last day at work." In other words, be ready to turn on a dime if the unexpected happens. Be prepared emotionally as well as financially. Have other irons in the fire.

## Be Loyal to Yourself

> "You have to recognize loyalty to yourself."
> —WES

Most of the people I spoke with professed great loyalty to their companies and believed that loyalty would be returned. As such, they did not look at other opportunities or spend much time networking outside their workplaces. After their experiences being let go, many acknowledged that they should have been more loyal to themselves.

In the book *The Alliance: Managing Talent in the Networked Age*, Reid Hoffman, cofounder and chair of LinkedIn, along with coauthors Ben Casnocha and Chris Yeh, begins by outlining what's wrong with modern-day employment.

> Imagine it's your first day of work at a new company. Your manager greets you with warm enthusiasm, welcomes you to the family, and expresses her hope that you'll be with the company for many years to come. Then she hands you off to the HR department, who sits you down in a conference room and spends thirty

minutes explaining that you're on a ninety-day probation period and that even after that, you'll be an "at will" employee. At any moment you can be fired. For any reason, you can be fired. Even if your boss has no reason at all, you can be fired.

You just experienced the fundamental disconnect of modern employment: the employer-employee relationship is based on a dishonest conversation.

Today, few companies offer guaranteed employment with a straight face; such assurances are perceived by employees as naïve, disingenuous, or both. Instead, employers talk about retention and tenure with fuzzy language: their goal is to retain "good" employees and the time frame is...indefinite. This fuzziness actually destroys trust—the company is asking employees to commit to itself without committing to them in return...

The old model of employment was a good fit for an era of stability. In stable times, companies grew larger to leverage economies of scale and process improvement. These titans offered an implicit deal to their workers: We provide lifelong employment in exchange for loyal service.

In that era, careers were considered nearly as permanent as marriage. Employers and employees committed to each other, for better or worse, through bull and bear markets, until retirement did them part. For white-collar professionals, progressing in one's career was like riding an escalator, with predictable advancement for those who followed the rules. Because both sides expected the relationship to be permanent, both sides were willing to invest in it and each other.

The traditional model of lifetime employment, so well-suited to periods of relative stability, is too rigid for today's networked age. Few American companies can provide the traditional career ladder for their employees anymore; the model is in varying degrees of disarray globally.

In her research on the unemployed, found in her book *The Tumbleweed Society*, Allison Pugh captures the phenomenon this way:

The one-way honor system is when individual workers profess having an intense work ethic that also involves loyalty or identifying with the employers. Many people that I interviewed said that they give :150 percent, or 100 percent, or 125 percent, so the individual is pledging themselves as a statement of personal character. They're saying, "I'm a good person, see how much I identify with work and can be relied on."

On the other hand, for the last 30 years or so, employers have been pulling away from making any similar pledge. And there's no blame for employers—even people who had been laid off said it's not the company's job to worry about workers, they have to be lean and mean in a tough economy. Americans appear to have entirely capitulated to the model of the high-performance company that doesn't owe anything to workers aside from, as one woman that I interviewed said, "a paycheck and some respect."

At his new position, Wes struggles with loyalty. "I guess even now I say loyalty and dedication—it's still just a job. Even now I put in fifty to sixty hours, and I question why I am doing it. It's just a job. Unless you have equity or ownership…you have to recognize loyalty to yourself."

Taking it a step further, Connie warned, "People have to be on the lookout for themselves. It's easy to get complacent."

Providing some specific suggestions, Randy asserted, "We have this stupid thing called loyalty. Work, work, work. Unfortunately, the only way to take care of yourself, *not your job*, is to gain contacts—out from behind your desk! Pay more attention to your own self as well as the organization."

The clear sentiment from most of the people I spoke to was this: *I gave 100 percent or more. I was loyal. I sacrificed. The company was not loyal in return.* Given that their loyalty was not returned, the people I interviewed stressed the importance of being loyal to oneself.

## Watch Out for Politics

"Stay out of the mix of things."
—ELIZABETH

The interviewees had strong opinions and advice about office politics and their impact on career survival. In fact, they saw a strong relationship between playing politics and keeping a job.

"We live in a volatile world where change is not the exception, it's the rule. Scan the environment no matter how things are going. Continually assess your environment," Nick advised. He pointed out that politics is sometimes a matter of who you are associated with. "I got caught before—I was on autopilot. I thought, 'I'm never going to have to interview for another job.' I was blind to the world around me. A four-year wait, watching my boss wait his turn, and then his boss hired a friend. Pay attention to the signals. What I used to laugh off, I take seriously now."

Gail also warned about office politics "I didn't get sucked into the drama, and I would advise people not to. Have a calm presence. Draw good, healthy boundaries between yourself and your colleagues. Be strategic about your relationships. You won't like everyone. You don't have to in order for them to be helpful to you. This was a mistake I made. I ended up not liking my boss. For me it became personal too. I probably started doing things that were evident to him. I should have detached myself from the personal part and been strategic about the work part. Keep a detached perspective and think about how they can help you or your career."

After losing her job, Diane admitted, "I became distrustful. I don't think I got to the point where I was comfortable with any leadership. Keep your cards close to the vest, keep your head down, do your best, and don't offer an opinion. Go home. Be guarded. Do what is best for you. Do not trust anyone. Do not stay anywhere for twenty-eight years. If you are going to work somewhere a long time, work where there is protection."

Connie compares workplace politics to the television reality show Survivor, warning that if you are in the wrong alliance you could lose your job. Like the high school, she notes we experience cliques all our lives, where in each group there is a pecking order in each group there's a pecking order.

Connie warns others, "Be careful who your enemies are. Be watchful of it. There are people you have to be careful of. They just aren't going to like you. You have to be cognizant of that. You have to be careful if you have a boss that's going to listen to it. You don't think that way; you are doing a good job. But if you have a boss that is going to listen to it, look out."

"You have to figure out who is in power and make them happy, or you will be on the cutting block. You have to play a game and make yourself valuable while you make your exit plan," Janice explained.

## Key Takeaways

1. Remind yourself that the days of long-term employment in a single organization are becoming rare.
2. Even if you are happy with your present job, keep your eyes and ears out for other opportunities. Be ready with a current résumé, including accomplishments, and an updated LinkedIn account.
3. Locate and read your employee handbook and any human resource policies you can find.
4. Be involved in professional and personal activities outside of work. It is key to establish a network before you need one.
5. Use your vacation time.
6. Be loyal to yourself.
7. Save your money.
8. Take care of your health and medical needs while you are employed.
9. Watch the workplace politics and environment carefully.

# CHAPTER 11

## ADVICE FROM THE FIRING LINE: TIPS FOR THOSE ACTIVELY SEEKING A JOB

In the best of circumstances, a job search is a tedious, humbling, and exhausting undertaking. The uncertainty and waiting are painful, and the rejections are demoralizing. For those out of work, the search carries with it even greater angst. The stakes are higher, much higher.

This chapter begins with stories of job search frustrations. I share these for two reasons: First, I believe readers who are in the throes of a job search may be able to relate to these stories and see that they are not alone in their struggles. Second, I hope readers can draw insights from them. For those of you who haven't experienced what it's like to be unemployed and looking for a job, this may shed light on what it's like to seek work. And for hiring managers, this may provide heightened sensitivity to your applicants' points of view.

The chapter concludes with advice for those seeking a job. While there are many books and resources on job seeking, some of which I have referenced, advice from those on the firing line may be the most relevant. The people I talked with genuinely hope you can learn from both their disappointments and successes.

## Job Search Woes

> "I felt I had to take action. I've had enough,
> and I'm not going to take this anymore."
> —JOE

Becoming unemployed sent a panic through several of the interviewees. Randy dedicated much of his time to a job search: "I'm spending almost eight hours a day working on finding another job, so there really hasn't been a lot of free time other than I don't have a two-hour daily commute. I'm not leaving anything to chance, so I spend significant time e-mailing and calling folks. It seems that I'm more anal about the whole looking-for-a-job thing than I would have guessed…make that *a lot more anal.* I am worried that if I took a job, a better one would come along. It might, but then again, it might not. I keep telling myself, 'Would I react any different if I were thirty-five instead of fifty-five?'" It took Randy over a year to find a full-time job in his field.

"It took me nine months to find a job—a long time," recalled Melissa. "And I didn't get close to my old salary. My unemployment ran out. I didn't care what anyone paid. I would take anything."

Melissa lamented the lack of responsiveness and feedback in her job search. "When you're someone like me who wants to improve, it's hard to go without feedback. I applied where I knew I was more qualified than many of their candidates, and when they said no, it was so hard. I wanted to know what I could do to improve." Melissa's experience is not unique. Typically applicants are not given feedback on why they didn't get the job. If an internal applicant was hired, the company may communicate that reason. At most, applicants get the usual response that someone was hired "whose skills and experience more closely matched the position's requirements."

Janice relayed some practical advice from her experience: "Don't expect to find an ideal job right away. Accept something you know you can do, even if it pays less. You've got to start somewhere. You have to build back up to show you can be successful as you were in the past. Or even try something totally new. A lot of people can use their talents in a new business where they could be happy and successful." Knowing it is easier to find a job when you are employed, Janice recommends getting back to work as soon as possible, even if the job isn't ideal.

Age was a factor in several of the interviewees' job seeking. Connie summarized the difficulty of finding a job as an older worker. "I applied for a couple jobs, but I didn't get them. They ended up hiring someone younger. They could get someone younger and cheaper who would work longer." Connie didn't find a full-time job; instead she started her own law practice.

Wes treated his job search as a full-time job, and it took him a year and four months to find a new position. He recalled, "There were some depressing points when you are a year out, and you try to deal with it. You keep plugging along."

Relocations were a necessary evil for some. Nick reported that it took him six months to find a job, and as he had anticipated, the job required him and his family to move. "I lived away from my family for three months so my daughter could graduate high school. I had lots of opportunities to interview and actually had a couple offers to choose from."

It took Julie ten months to find a job at a counseling center. She says she was lucky: she became aware of someone resigning, she applied, and she got the job.

Two stories in particular drive home how challenging and frustrating the job search process can be. Don and Joe both experienced great anxiety and hardship in finding a job. Their stories below are poignant reminders of how we all can be more sensitive to the challenges of unemployment.

Don was out of work in his field for six months. He described this painful period: "I couldn't even get an interview. *I would do anything— anything to support my family.* I drove a truck. I went to work for my brother splitting logs, living away from my family. I hated it. I had to do it. I had to support my family. Do you know how hard logging is? Splitting logs is back-breaking work. After you cut down the tree and split the logs, you have to load them on the truck one by one. I was glad for the work, but it was hard. Plus the trees are covered with green moss. At the end of the day, you'd be covered with it.

"One day after work I was covered in moss and dirt from head to toe, I smelled, and I was filthy. I walked out of the woods toward the street. I saw a parked car. I peered in the window. On the passenger seat was a briefcase and a lunch bag. I thought to myself, 'That guy is going to work in his cube and taking his lunch to work. *I used to be that guy.*' I so wanted to be that guy again. He had my life. I used to think it would be great if I didn't have to work in a cubicle and pack my lunch. I wanted that life again." His angst is palpable. Can't you just picture him looking through the car window, covered in moss and dirt, longing for the life he used to have?

Frustration and feeling powerless drove Joe to the breaking point. Fortunately, he had enough sense to reach out for help. After searching more than a year for work, he decided to try looking in a new field. He interviewed for a leadership position out of town. "They offered me a job. My wife needed to see the area first. We went and looked at neighborhoods and schools. I remember sharing with her that I was reluctant take a job in a new field. The day after we returned from our trip, I got *another* opportunity. I was one of two final candidates. The next step in that interview process was to do psychological testing. I went for the testing. Then I got a call from the company that first offered me a job. They asked me where I was. I told them I was taking a test for a different position I had applied for.

"I was honest and not savvy. They were angry and rescinded the offer they made me for the position. The position I was testing for didn't work out either. Then I was back to looking for jobs, interviewing." Joe admitted his naiveté. His honesty about looking at a different job after being offered one resulted in the job offer being rescinded.

"I was getting pissed off. I had a job offer, and then I made a mistake and they rescinded it. I thought to myself, 'I am going to talk to this guy and ask him to reconsider. I flew out to the company on my own dime. I felt I had to take action. *I've had enough, and I'm not going to take this anymore.*"

Joe was desperate. "I flew to the company that offered me the job instead of going to the headhunter appointment that my former CEO set up for me. I drove right to the office building and thought I should first call the man who rescinded the job offer rather than just drop in. I called, and he would not see me. He threatened to call security if I came on the grounds.

"I went to a restaurant and thought. I called my wife and told her about it. I called a pastor friend who just got a church in the area. I called him and told him what happened. He picked me up and took me to his new church. He could tell I was despondent. I could hear him talking to my wife on another phone. Both of them were trying to figure out how to get me home. I thought the pastor was going to try to commit me, but he assured me he was just trying to get me home."

Joe flew home, and his father-in-law picked him up at the airport. "I needed to get help. I got a psychiatrist. I look at that time as so difficult. 'I am going to find a job. I am going to take action.' Out of that came, 'I am going to get support.' I had bottomed out.

"It was a turning point. I started running again. I saw the psychiatrist. I was back out networking. I was twelve months out of work. I called my old boss and asked for three months more of outplacement counseling. He agreed. Again I made calls, made lists. That led to interviews, and I eventually got work."

The job search process is time-consuming, deflating, and full of uncertainties. Most of the people I interviewed took more than six months to find a job. Worried about supporting their families, Don and Joe were brought to the brink of desperation and panic. Their job search woes consumed and demoralized them. In Joe's case, his desperation led to several mistakes in judgment, one of which cost him a job. His need to take action led to an attempt at confronting the person who rescinded the job offer. Fortunately, Joe sought help and eventually found work.

## The Challenges of Electronic Applications and Applicant Tracking Systems

> "Just tell me…yes, no, I don't care. Just let me know. They are so slow. What are they doing?"
> —RANDY

If you are looking for work, be prepared to fill out your job application online. The online employment application process is time-consuming, tedious, and by some accounts, a waste of time for the job seeker. The application will ask you to complete a detailed job history, and the website will likely require you to upload your résumé. Participants reported that the process typically took two hours.

Some systems do not allow the users to save their work. Participants in the study reported that while filling out online applications, they needed to stop to obtain a driver's license or an address. When they returned to the computer, they were locked out and all their information was lost.

"I don't know how to apply for all these jobs," Melissa complained. "You don't hear back, so you feel like a loser. I found out how little HR departments know about how to use computers and Internet searches. So they can't find qualified candidates either."

Randy said he sent out sixty-five to seventy résumés. He expressed anger and frustration about not getting responses. "Just tell me…yes, no, I don't care. Just let me know. They are so slow. What are they doing?" He applied for positions that were considerably below his last several jobs and at considerably lower pay.

Experts cast great doubt on the effectiveness of electronic applicant tracking systems for job seekers. In his article "Why You Can't Get a Job… Recruiting Explained by the Numbers," Dr. John Sullivan states, "For the specific case of an online job posting, on average, 1,000 individuals will see a job post, 200 will begin the application process, 100 will complete the application, 75 of those 100 resumes will be screened out by either the ATS or a recruiter, 25 resumes will be seen by the hiring manager, 4 to 6 will be invited for an interview, 1 to 3 of them will be invited back for final interview, 1 will be offered that job and 80 percent of those receiving an offer will accept it."

Allison Doyle from the *Balance* reports that applicant tracking systems are used to screen candidates as well. They work by scanning résumés and applications, looking for keywords. The keywords for each job are unique as they relate back to the qualifications and experience needed for a particular job.

"One way an ATS works is to eliminate résumés that are missing certain keywords. If the software or the hiring manager does not detect any of the keywords in your résumé or cover letter, your application might get thrown out. By embedding keywords in your résumé or cover letter, you will demonstrate, at a glance, that you fit the requirements of the position," she advises.

Dr. Sullivan describes a common error that job seekers make. "I estimate more than 90 percent of candidates apply using their standard résumé (without any customization). Unfortunately, this practice dramatically increases the odds that a résumé will be instantly rejected because a résumé that is not customized to the job will seldom include enough of the required 'keywords' to qualify for the next step, a review by a human." For best results, tailor each résumé to the job you are seeking, highlighting how your background and credentials are a match for what the company is looking for.

Looking back on her experience with ATS systems, Melissa acknowledged, "I wasn't prepared for this new way of getting your résumé even looked at. I didn't know about the keyword search. Sending it in electronically and not getting anything back, going months without hearing anything, then that was even more depressing."

The lack of results from applying for jobs online was troubling to Don. "I relentlessly applied for work. I applied en masse for up to twenty jobs at a time, all for nothing."

Many experts suggest that the best way to overcome the challenges of an ATS system is to obtain a referral from someone on the inside. The importance of this cannot be overstated. Remember that dozens of applications are submitted electronically for each position. Having an employee of the company suggest to the hiring manager or human resources to take a look at your résumé will improve your odds. Managers appreciate knowing someone can vouch for you. The hiring process is tedious and overwhelming for them as well. Your application is now more likely to be considered, especially if your contact is a valued employee.

In her online *US News and World Report* article "Don't Believe These 8 Job Search Myths," Hannah Morgan writes, "You may believe that if you apply to enough jobs, you'll eventually beat the odds and land one. While applying to jobs may make you feel productive, a recent CareerXroads survey shows that only 15 percent of positions were filled through job boards. Most jobs are either filled internally or through referrals."

## Résumés

Résumés are a key marketing tool for job seekers. Many of the interviewees obtained professional help in developing their résumés and would recommend the same to others. Some used career counselors or outplacement specialists; some hired freelance résumé writers.

Résumé writing may be as much art as science. Randy sought out assistance from two different outplacement counselors for his résumé. "I spent an hour today on the phone with another career coach, who told me my résumé, which another professional already redid, wasn't formatted correctly, and it's no wonder I've not been placed yet. I kept thinking the whole time, I could do what she's doing, and so what the hell's wrong with me anyway!"

Gail sought help from a freelance writer for her résumé and learned that the traditional format for a résumé is no longer in fashion. "Résumé writing has evolved so quickly—now you keep it sparse and powerful. You use color and call out boxes. It has to be visually appealing. It's more like a marketing brochure. The résumé is supposed to reflect your story, who you are, not just what you have done."

Whatever the length or look, résumés need to be customized to the job you are looking for. According to a study by TheLadders, recruiters spend an average of six seconds on a résumé.

Referring to this study, Dr. John Sullivan states in "Why You Can't Get a Job": "Having a clear or professionally organized résumé format that presents relevant information where recruiters expect it will improve the rating of a résumé by recruiter by a whopping 60 percent, without any change to the content (a 6.2 versus a 3.9 usability rating [on a scale of 1–7] for the less-professionally organized.)"

You must carefully examine the job qualifications each employer seeks and then depict in the résumé how your qualifications match the job. It should go without saying—it is a mistake to have one résumé and submit it to any job you are looking for. Dr. John Sullivan offers some helpful advice after you've completed your enhanced résumé: "But next comes the most important step: to literally 'pretest' both your résumé and your LinkedIn profile several times with a recruiter or HR professional. Pretesting makes sure that anyone who scans them for six seconds will be able to actually find each of the key points that recruiters need to find.

## Interviews Gone Wrong

> "My confidence was shaken. I walked
> out, and I knew I blew it."
> —SONDRA

Getting to an interview is the first step for a job seeker. Job searches require that people get through the interview process. Several of the people I talked with had bad experiences with interviews.

For example, Julie had her share of challenges with job interviews. "I had lots of disappointing job interviews for any type of job. I was too qualified for some, not qualified for others. I tried some temporary work. It's a weird spot to be in: too qualified or not enough. Let down after let down."

The beginning of Sondra's job search was rough, "I started responding to job ads. I had an interview, but it was too soon after I was fired. I tore myself apart. They would ask me something, and I'd say, 'I don't know if I can do that.' They would talk about doing work in teams. 'I don't think I can do this.' My confidence was shaken. I walked out, and I knew I blew it." Sondra had panicked. Interviewing with confidence and poise is difficult when your confidence is shaken.

Randy had an unusual interview experience, or as it turned out, lack of interview. A company asked him to come for an interview in another region of the country. He and his wife drove there the day before. The next morning, they had breakfast together. He then left to get to his interview in plenty of time. On his way there, he got a call that informed him they weren't interviewing anyone. "Someone up the food chain decided they wanted an internal person. And they forgot to call me. My wife and I just turned around and drove home. So we can say we went cross-country for breakfast. Unbelievable."

Those I interviewed talked about getting their hopes up after several interviews only to be disappointed. Wes shared, "I was out about a year and three to four months. There were a few second and third interviews, so I thought the chances were good. It's a numbers game, I guess. I was just fifty; that could have been a factor. I don't think it helps, but it's not a terrible hindrance."

## Freelancing

According to Barbara Mistick and Karie Willyerd, authors of the book *How to Future-Proof Yourself for Tomorrow's Workplace*, experts claim that contract work now makes up 30 percent of the workforce. In their study, Mistick and Willyerd learned that 83 percent of executives around the world intend to use more contract, contingent, or flex workers in the future. This presents an opportunity for job seekers to become known to a company through contract work. Freelancing bridged the pay and work gap for several people while they were looking for full-time work. For others, freelancing became their next career.

In his late fifties when he lost his job, Paul was in the insurance field. He was out of full-time work for two years and did as much consulting as he could during that time. Eventually he found a full-time job with one of his clients. Had he not been known to the company through his consulting work, Paul believes he would not have gotten the job or even been selected to interview for it.

Elizabeth also tapped into her network to find some interim work. "I got some consulting work thanks to some former colleagues," she explained. "I filled in for someone on medical leave. My husband admired them and thanked them for offering me the consulting. They stepped up when I lost my job." While she eventually found full-time work, she continued to do part-time consulting for her former colleagues.

While Paul and Elizabeth did freelance work until they found full-time jobs, Connie and Mark turned their job losses into full-time contract work. Connie shared, "I got interviews because my former boss did me a favor. One of the interviews was with the city. They went with someone younger, but they hired me to do investigations for them. It's better to be a consultant, and you don't have to deal with the politics."

At his wife's encouragement, Mark started freelancing. "I got an attorney and set up an LLC. That was scary. I read as much as I could. I was worried about the taxes, liability. There's a lot to worry about. You are your own travel agent, secretary, and scheduler. When I had clients, there was no downtime. That was fun but hard—living out of a hotel, flying, driving. I felt back in my element. I was producing and helping people. It makes me feel good when people ask for my help."

Freelancing is both a means to an end and an end in itself. Freelancing allows you to bridge an employment gap and keep your skills active. It's a way to get to know different businesses. It also provides a way to make money. Freelancing can be a filler for the résumé gap resulting from a job loss. In some cases, freelancing can lead to full-time employment. In others it can lead to a new career.


## Advice for Job Seekers


## Self-Reflection and Assessment

> "What do I want to do?"
> —CONNIE

Although an unwelcome event for most, losing a job gives you the opportunity to reflect on what you would like to do next, and many of the interviewees did just that. Several people described the event as a chance to examine their lives and their strengths and weaknesses. They acknowledged that the job loss gave them an opportunity to really think about what they wanted.

Gail is a good example of this. "I thought a lot about what I wanted to do next; I knew it needed to be out of the sandbox. I did give it some thought. I did journaling. That was good. It lifted my brain and kept me thinking about a future career. I gave it a lot of thought. I was noodling it."

Like Gail, Mark saw his job loss as an opportunity for self-assessment. "A good thing to ask is, 'What do I want to do when I grow up? What am I good at?' I didn't know if I had the gumption to go back to the hospitality industry. I even weighed the values of being a Walmart greeter and that it's not a good use of my time. It's a travesty. I went to Arby's. A part-time worker makes $7.45 an hour. That's ridiculous. So I would tell people, what are you willing to do? Do you have enough resources where you could go back to school? Look at your strengths and weaknesses."

Connie too went through the process of sorting out what she would like to do next. "I did go through the thinking, 'What do I want to do?' I told myself, 'I will do something.' Then I went back to my own profession. I like being able to set my own hours." Although she returned to her profession, this time Connie opened her own practice instead of working for a corporation.

It wasn't an easy path, but Diane used her job loss to start a new career. While working at her new full-time job, she returned to college and pursued a new degree. "I got my master's and finished my teaching license. I am now teaching. Losing my job took me in a new direction. I was determined it would not define me."

Nick also suggested a self-assessment, "Deal with it however you and your family have to deal with it. Ask yourself what you want to do next. I knew what I didn't want to do. What do I really want to do?

## Looking for a Job Is a Full-time Job

> "I think your job search kind of becomes your job."
> —Wes

"Looking for a new position is a full-time job. It's painful to be job seeking, but it's better than being in that environment," Randy said, referring to his former company.

Nick recalled, "I was really focused on getting a job. I got up every day, shaved, showered, and set up my laptop, networked, and applied for jobs—all day. I treated it like a full-time job. It takes a while. You don't apply and get interviewed and start a week later. It's a three-month process at least. Even if I had an interview one place, I kept looking."

## Clean Up Your Online Presence

In her article "How to Bounce Back After Being Fired" on the Women's Health website, Kate Sullivan says: "A survey found that 38 percent of laid-off or fired workers bad-mouthed their former employer, in many cases on the Internet. 'No company sees complaints about your last job on Twitter and thinks, 'Oh, we've got to get some of that on our team!' says Jon Acuff, author of *Do Over: Rescue Monday, Reinvent Your Work, and Never Get Stuck*. And they will see it: Ninety-three percent of recruiters say they look at a candidate's social media profiles."

Whether online or in conversation, it's never a good idea to bad-mouth your former employer. The night Julie was fired, she wrote a long diatribe on her Facebook page, lambasting her former employer, who she named in the post, and expressing her emotions—pain, anger, confusion—for all to see. A former colleague messaged her saying she understood her anger, but suggested she take down the post. Julie took the advice to heart and removed the post, thanking her former colleague for the advice.

Bruce, Gail, Wes, and Andrew all described how they got help improving their LinkedIn profile. The importance of LinkedIn cannot be overestimated. Recruiters and headhunters mine the data on LinkedIn to find qualified candidates. According to TheLadders, "Because many recruiters and hiring managers use LinkedIn profiles either to verify or to supplement résumé information, those profiles also impact your chances. Eye-tracking technology used by TheLadders revealed that recruiters spend an average of 19 percent of their time on your LinkedIn profile simply viewing your picture (so a professional picture may be worthwhile).

## Put Your Best Foot Forward

It might be difficult, but don't let being let go be an excuse for letting yourself go. Although it's understandable that you may lack the motivation to take care of yourself, it is important to do so. Paula shared, "One of the things I realized was that I could run into someone at any time who could help me get a job, or someone who I might ask to be a reference, or someone who could introduce me to someone. That meant I had to look my best all the time. I couldn't run to the grocery store in my sweats anymore. I had to do my hair every day. Now I'm not saying I wore a suit to go to Publix; I am just saying that I had to be ready at any time to run into people who could help me. It's hard when you feel your worst to look your best. But I had to."

Many studies confirm an interview bias toward people who are more fit and better looking. Exercising regularly is advised. Exercise will help you combat the emotional impact of being unemployed and provide you with needed energy to put toward your job search. And appearing physically fit may convey qualities like self-discipline and a strong work ethic.

Looking your best is important, so is presenting yourself to others in a positive way. While it is difficult, it is worth the effort.

## Network

> "Network, network, network."
> —ANDREW

The United States Department of Labor gives some startling statistics about how jobs are found:

- 70 percent through networking, i.e., through personal and professional contacts
- 15 percent through search firms (mostly managerial positions, not entry level)
- 10–12 percent through want ads/classified ads

- 4 percent by people going into business for themselves and creating their own jobs
- 2 percent by blindly sending out résumés

One thing you could take from these statistics is that you should spend at least 70 percent of your job-search time on nurturing relationships through networking, since that is the most likely source of found jobs. Your network is not limited to your closest circle of friends and family. It also includes former coworkers, fellow church members, parents of the kids on your child's soccer team, neighbors and acquaintances, and their families and friends.

In his landmark study, Mark Granovetter, a sociologist at Stanford University, demonstrated the strength of "weak ties." His research showed that people were more likely to find jobs through weak ties—friends of friends—than through strong ties, close friends, and family. To underscore the importance of networking, according to Cornell University's Career Center, 80 percent of available jobs aren't even advertised. These jobs are often referred to as the hidden job market.

Many of the interviewees found jobs through their network. Melissa summarized the feelings of many: "You feel so guarded that it's hard to do." But this is an important finding, because while networking may be uncomfortable for some, it is *effective*. The following stories bring this effectiveness to even greater light.

Sondra began her job search by renewing former contacts. "While I was in college, I interviewed with a guy named Ken. He wanted to hire me then but didn't think the job was right for me. When I got fired after three months, I called Ken and let him know I was available. He didn't ask too many questions, but he did wonder why I was available. I told him it wasn't a good fit, and he seemed OK with that. He told me there was a job in the works, but it wouldn't be available for a couple months. I started there three months after I got fired. I love it. I am making much more money, and I am really happy."

Networking also worked for Elizabeth. Here is her experience: "I got this full-time job from a friend who worked at an organization and got me involved. I intended to do consulting for the organization, not work full time. Later when I met with them, they were so impressed, they offered me a full-time job. But it wasn't what I was making before. And then they fired the person who brought me to them. So I began to look again." Elizabeth's next position was also found through networking. A former coworker who Elizabeth had stayed in touch with moved to a new organization and hired her.

Out of work for more than a year, Wes used the services of an outplacement firm. He thought back on all the work involved in his job search, only to find a job through someone he grew up with: "After I had done all these searches, a good friend of mine said the guy he did insurance for was looking for a CFO/controller for his company. And two weeks later I got a job."

Andrew sings the praises of networking. He emphatically advises that everyone should *"network, network, and network!"* Andrew didn't spend a lot of time thinking about networking before he was laid off. "But I think about it all the time now."

Likewise, Joe says, "Do the networking, and keep up your network." He warns against thinking, "I'm good; I don't need to be networking. Everyone will want me."

Renee recalled how an acquaintance from college had heard she had to reapply for her job and was at risk of losing it. He worked at the same company in a different department, and he told her he had a job available. So she interviewed with him and got the job.

After she was fired, job search success came to Diane through networking. "I reached out to a person who used to work with me. She was now at another human services agency serving the same population. She told me about a position there. It wasn't a leadership position, and it was less money. It was a job, it was peaceful, and they valued me. The biggest piece of advice I have is network and get the word out. Call everyone you can think of to let them know you're available."

One interviewee's experience illustrates Granovetter's strength of weak ties theory. Karen interviewed for a position to run a small membership association but didn't get the job. "Six months later one of the board members who interviewed me contacted me through LinkedIn. He said a headhunter reached out to him to see if he could recommend someone for a senior-level position in my field. He asked me if he could pass my name along. Of course I said yes. The headhunter contacted me and set up an interview. He brought me in to meet the executive team of the organization, and I got the job."

Gail too had an impressive experience with the strength of weak ties. She said she wasn't really looking for what "fell in her lap," but it was absolutely the right opportunity at the right time. "My niece, who worked at a major consulting firm, asked me to meet with one of the partners. The partner was attending a conference and needed some background information about my area of expertise. I met the partner for lunch. She sat down and abruptly said, 'I only have forty-five minutes.' I told her to eat and I'd talk. I walked her through the field, the emerging trends. An hour and a half later, she offered me a job. I wasn't ready to accept, so she offered to call me in a month. She did. She was very close with my niece and called her, saying, "I found the person to start our new practice area."

"You never know. I was just doing a favor for my niece. It came out of the blue. Never, never ignore something that is *out of the blue*. The blue is actually a place. The blue is often your destiny calling you. If something is out of the blue, it could be your destiny."

Gail has some specific suggestions for networking: "Build your external network. Nurture it. Have the lunches, join the boards, volunteer. Extract yourself from the organization so you have a network to go to when you leave your organization. The organization becomes your family. I was fortunate that my role was about the external network. I had a network in place. A lot of people don't. Women spend too much time nurturing the internal network and not enough on the external. Anchor yourself in a broader network."

Everyone is a potential reference, introduction, coworker, or boss. You never know. Gail had not even begun her job search when her niece asked for her help. She had no forethought whatsoever that she would be meeting her next employer. Renee had no idea that a colleague would offer her a job and a soft landing. After all his job-seeking activities, Wes was surprised that a childhood friend connected him with one of his clients who was looking for a CFO.

## Outplacement Career Counseling

"Go to a career counselor."
—JULIE

Several of the people interviewed sought help from a career counselor or an outplacement firm. Sondra sought assistance from her college's career advising office. "My career counselors helped me build a framework for how to explain my getting fired. They gave me clear-cut steps. They told me I can explain it wasn't a good fit. They encouraged me to talk about what I want moving forward in a job in a way that was productive." It is important to practice answering the question of why you left your last employer concisely and confidently and without bad-mouthing your former company. Working with a career counselor gave Sondra the confidence and tools to be successful in her job search.

Sometimes outplacement services are offered by a company with layoffs or other forms of job cuts. Andrew was grateful for the help he received from his outplacement firm. Support came in the form of classes and individual conversations with a consultant. His counselors explained the job-search process and helped him handle the stress. He took part in four- to five-hour courses that focused on all aspects of the job-search process, including "how to answer difficult interview questions, explain in every answer what you can do for the company, and pull together little stories that tie into your attributes and skills to show you're ready to go."

Andrew emphasized the counselors' assistance with practicing answers to interview questions in the right way. "For each question they want you to turn it into a solution for them. Even if it's 'tell me about yourself,' tailor it into what you can do for them. They teach you how to interview, how to speak to others. I learned a lot. These things are not taught anywhere else and not practiced anywhere else, but you absolutely need to develop that skill to succeed."

The outplacement firm stressed another component: building and contacting your network. They reinforced the need to have those interactions while avoiding looking desperate. Andrew said, "Focus on telling your story."

All of those who used outplacement services mentioned their help and recommendations in building a social media presence, including a professional head shot and high-level profile on LinkedIn.

While it didn't have any direct impact on his getting a job, Wes had a positive experience with outplacement services. "I would say to get outplacement services—individual coaching, résumé writing, office space, being a part of a group, and having a place to go is helpful. I participated in one or two other groups that got together and got their input. Going through the paces of interviewing and writing letters is helpful."

While Julie, Sondra, Wes, and Andrew found their experiences with career counselors helpful, Randy was not as positive. He found that outplacement counselors could give competing advice. He had one career coach redo his résumé only to be told by another professional that it wasn't formatted correctly and that was the reason he hadn't been placed yet.

Often with layoffs or other terminations, outplacement services will be offered. Several people I interviewed sought out the assistance of a career counselor or outplacement services and would recommend these services to others, especially when the company is providing them.

## Keep the Faith

> "You are going to get through it."
> —DIANE

The people I interviewed knew firsthand the challenges of looking for work and how demoralizing it can be. Yet they also offered some encouragement. Elizabeth reminds job seekers to press forward and rely on their faith: "Don't give up. Just keep looking. Keep looking. Keep faith. Strong faith will help you get through."

Likewise, Lori encourages job seekers not to give up on themselves. "You might have been treated poorly, but it doesn't reflect on who you are and what you bring to the workplace. Whatever you are feeling, it's OK. Deal with whatever emotion you wake up with each morning; try to put it in perspective. You do have to grieve. It's like the loss of a loved one. That's OK. If you need time alone, that's OK."

Diane tells others in the same boat, "You are going to get through it. You will get through this, and you will be better than you were because you survived."

Even through the difficulty of unemployment, Don counted his blessings: "When I began to realize I wasn't making any progress and my faith was low, the Lord provided a solid engineering job just twelve miles from our home. This meant I could joyfully return to my family, our church, and a somewhat normal life! I was so blessed."

## Key Takeaways

1. Remember, 70 percent of jobs are found through networking.
2. Take advantage of outplacement assistance if your employer provides it.
3. If you are sending in online applications, it helps to find someone who works there to recommend that the hiring manager look at your application.
4. Have someone help you practice interviewing.
5. Maintain your health and your appearance.
6. Freelancing might be a bridge to new employment or a new career.
7. Keep the faith.

# CHAPTER 12

## BURN SCARS: HOW GETTING FIRED CHANGES PEOPLE

S ignificant life events leave their marks on us. I was interested in learning how people were impacted by the experience of losing a job. I asked the interviewees to reflect on their experiences and share how they have been shaped by them. Were they different now and, if so, how did they change?

### Connecting with Others

> "I will be different; I will be supportive of
> people looking for a better job too."
> —RANDY

One of the most common findings was that those interviewed developed a heightened sense of the importance of relationships. On a personal or professional front, the loss of a job made them realize the importance of connecting with others, helping others, and being there for others.

Profoundly impacted by her first two job losses, Brenda recommitted herself to being intentional about relationships. She shared that on a personal level if she even thinks about someone, she will connect with them. "I am going to reach out. That's the promise I made myself."

On a professional level, interviewees related that they were more likely to connect as well. Andrew said he has a much different perspective on his whole career progression as well as networking. "I didn't spend a lot of time thinking about networking before, but I think about it all the time now." He now keeps in touch with people across his work life and makes it a point to share job opportunities with others, "Have you heard about such- and-such opportunity?"

Many also had developed more empathy for those seeking employment. Randy shared, "It's a learning experience—that puts it mildly. I will be approaching people differently. One thing is when people call me looking for a job or contact, I will respond quicker. People are grabbing for something. I will be different; I will be supportive of people looking for a better job too. I will support people and encourage them to do their networking."

Like Randy, Nick too says he is more responsive to people: "I now take calls. I return a call to anyone who calls me. For *myself* too, I return calls. I want to be appropriate. I connect with them." He also shared that he is more receptive to headhunters: "I learn a lot talking to headhunters. I think most of the ones I know are very successful and I can learn."

## The Job Is Not Me, My Identity

> "If your job is how you define yourself,
> when it's gone, who are you?"
> —BRENDA

In addition to putting more emphasis on connecting with others, the people I interviewed were intentional about separating their jobs from their identities. Brenda explained, "Well, I always defined myself by my job. I threw myself into the job—my total being—and moved up the ladder quickly. I just flew into this. I was a mover and shaker. So I defined myself by my job. And when that stopped the first and second time, it's like saying who you are. If that's how you define yourself, when it's gone, who are you? With age and wisdom, I truly know my heart. A job is not who I am. I am a good friend. I am a caring person. I knew it was important for people to connect with me."

Wes struggles to put his new job into perspective. "It's still just a job. Even now I put in fifty to sixty hours, and I question why I am doing it. It's just a job. Unless you have equity or ownership…you have to recognize loyalty to yourself."

After losing her job, Elizabeth recognized that she had spent too much of her time on the job and not enough with her family. "The job doesn't own you. It's just a means for you to make money to do what you want. *I can't wrap my whole world around a job again.* I was married to my computer and not my husband. My husband would say, 'You are married to that computer.' I found I have to take time for my family and not just focus on my job."

Joe admitted that separating work from who he is as a man is a struggle: "Finding a job is work, but I need work with intrinsic value. Men feel that when they aren't working, they aren't contributing and therefore not worthy. I know for me that my worth is tied up in work. To be not working is a real difficult thing for me."

For many, a job provides more than an income. It also provides status and role identity. Losing a job caused many of those interviewed to reflect on the role of work in their lives.

## Guarded, Fearful, and Insecure

> "I will never mistake a team for a family."
> —MELISSA

The expression "once bitten, twice shy" applies to these interviewees. A common thread among them is their feeling of being more guarded and distrustful at work. Lesley is a good example of this. "I'm probably more selective in what I do and who I do it for and with. I am definitely more guarded. I am leery. I am concerned with how I will be accepted."

Likewise, Melissa is careful not to let her guard down. "I am more guarded now about who I will let in at work. My true friends are my true friends. I do have lasting friends from work. But I am very guarded. I tell myself I will never do that again," she said, referring to how she let her personal and professional lives intertwine.

"Look at my husband—he hung pictures, moved furniture, helped decorate the office. He loved that I was working there. Treat them like family or like a team—that's a line I will never cross again. When you're out, you're out. I will never mistake a team for a family."

Friendships can also be tested and broken. Julie regretted becoming good friends with her supervisor and as a result has taken a new approach to relationships at work. "I am absolutely different. I am more mature. I don't take relationships at work past a professional level now. I keep all my work separate."

"I will never trust any company again," Diane declared. "I felt like a complete and utter ass. It used to be an honorable company. They trashed my reputation. I became distrustful. I don't think I got to the point where I was comfortable with any leadership. I try to keep things close to the vest, keep my head down, do my best, don't offer an opinion, and then go home. I'm guarded." Diane still felt the impact of the betrayal that ended her twenty-eight years of service and personal investment in her organization.

Janice admits she lost confidence after her job loss. "I don't have the same comfort level where I believe people think I know what I am talking about. It isn't as comfortable, but it's not uncomfortable."

Unfortunately, Lori shared that the experience of being fired has affected her confidence: "I would say that I have always had a fear of failing. After experiencing failure, I am less willing to put myself out there to fail. It enhanced my fear of failure. I have not gone back to managing people in the way I did when I was let go."

The feeling of being on thin ice is common among people who have been let go. The insecurity and sense of uncertainty is pervasive. Nick described how different he is after losing his job: "I never feel safe. I realize how naïve I was, how fortunate and blessed I have been."

With great sadness, Don told of his insecure feeling of having no permanency and how it has impacted his life. "We live in a beautiful home, but I realize it all can become a garage sale tomorrow. I don't even want to improve our home, thinking it's not permanent. I'd be spending my energies building something for another man I don't even know." Don's insecurity was compounded by the fear that he may end up like his father, who died in poverty.

Reacting to this fear, Don explained that he is more aggressive at work: "Outwardly I show confidence and leadership, while being inwardly I'm fearful and double-thinking my every move. I no longer say, 'We did it this way at my former employer.' I work harder out of fear. I am loyal and dedicated."

Wes stated simply his new reality. "An employee is expendable—be it at a fifty-employee company or a Fortune 500 company."

Recognizing the insecurity of employment, Joe said, "I take every opportunity to not take anything for granted." He realizes his life could turn on a dime.

## Radar Up

The interviewees stated that following their job loss, they became much more in tune to their environment, paying attention to any clues that might signal an impending job loss. "Now I hear everything differently," Nick stated. "If my boss says it's a good thing we're renting, I don't laugh it off. If he is taking calls from other places, while I feel comfortable and I get outstanding evaluations, I have no reason to believe I am going to work and live here the rest of my life." Clues Nick might have ignored before he was let go, he takes very seriously now.

Bruce had ignored the blatant warning signs and reflected on what he would do differently: "I think I would go with my gut more. A colleague warned me about my new boss. All I could say was, 'I can work with anyone.' But no, I couldn't. I should have listened to my colleague."

Joe related how he had changed through four job losses. "With each change I became savvier. I had a résumé in place. With each loss, the length of time out of work became less. I'm not questioning myself as much. I am more astute about how organizations work and networking, and I am not hesitant to seek help when other changes occur. I have sought help on each occasion. I have to get outside myself."

## Faith

A few people I spoke with found that their faith in God deepened as a result of being let go. "We are more dependent on the Lord for our family's provision," shared Don. Similarly, Lori said, "It has enhanced my faith. My needs were always met when they needed to be. It always happened that it worked out."

Reaffirming the relationships and connections in their lives and leaning on faith are two of the more positive changes people have experienced after being let go. However, the distrust is strong, and they are alert to any signs in their workplaces that it may happen again. Feelings of powerlessness, uncertainty, and insecurity last long after the interviewees lost their jobs and continued even after they found new ones. The result is a detachment from their jobs and their professional personas and clearer boundaries between their personal and professional lives.

And this may be the downside of employee engagement. Those in this study identified themselves as engaged, loyal, and dedicated. Most did not seek out other job opportunities and believe they sacrificed their personal time and interests for the best interest of the company. They expected that this engagement would be recognized and valued in return.

As workers experience or witness ungracious or unexpected terminations, they compensate by detaching and distrusting. As Gallup Daily poll reveals on March 5, 2017, only 33 percent of workers in America were engaged at work, meaning only a third of the nation's workers feel an emotional connection to their companies. Perhaps businesses and leaders attempting to create an engaged workplace culture should consider the impact of employee terminations on the remaining workforce when trying to build an engaged culture.

## Key Takeaways

1. Being fired often leaves lasting scars.
2. For many, losing a job means the loss of a sense of permanence and stability.
3. Becoming more guarded and distrustful at work is a common result of involuntary job loss.
4. People cope by engaging less at work and realizing their jobs don't define them.
5. Stay connected to the people in your life who love and support you.
6. As with any life crisis, getting counseling may be beneficial.

# CHAPTER 13

## LESSONS LEARNED FROM THE FIRING LINE: WHAT A JOB LOSS TEACHES US

I asked the participants what lessons they had learned on their journeys. This chapter includes the responses from the most frequently quoted people in this book, organized by individual rather than theme so you can see the full response. I also thought you would like to know how things turned out for them. So, after their comments, I included a "where they are now" summary.

### Brenda

First, I learned to stay true to who I am. If you know who you are and what's important to you, you can live with yourself. Second, stay true to your ethics. Even though you may not have value according to one person anymore, even though you don't have value to them, you still have value. Dig deep and find where that sits. I know I add value to my profession. Stay open to the answer. And third, you are not in control; God has to keep slapping you until you listen. He does have a better plan. I have been the calmest in my life the last fourteen years. Inner calm. That peace that's in your gut. It doesn't mean I don't get busy. I say, "Peace. Do what you can today; tomorrow there is more." Frame it as: How important is this? Once I realized I still had value, I could land on my feet and actually do better. Those are some of my lessons.

Brenda remains happily employed in the field she loves.

## Connie

What it made me realize is that you have to understand you are making enemies. And you don't even realize you are doing it. Just because someone is incompetent doesn't mean he or she won't end up in a position of power. Just because you are competent and clients like you doesn't mean you will be valued.

It's like the show *Survivor*—you could get in the wrong alliance and lose your job. Politics is politics, people are people. Just like the grade school playground, just like high school cliques. That's what you experience all your life. We are not a classless society. In each group there's a pecking order and gender issues.

Be careful who your enemies are. Be watchful of it. There are people you have to be careful of. They just aren't going to like you. You have to be cognizant of that. You have to be careful if you have a boss that's going to listen to it. You don't think that way; you are doing a good job. But if you have a boss that is going to listen to it, look out. If the boss isn't going anywhere, you could be in a bad fit. You have to move on.

Who would have thought? People are just bad news. Not everyone thinks about what's good for the company. They want to get rid of people. If they are secure, they like people who are competent who make them look good. If they are insecure, they have to get rid of that person.

There is nothing worse than politics. It's not "What have you done for me," it's "What have you done for me *today.*"

Connie opened her own law practice and has clients from many of the contacts she made while at the law firm.

194

## Randy

I learned my lesson about assessing situations and people. I missed this one when I interviewed or went there. I didn't see the warning signs coming from people who didn't want the change they said they wanted. It's all about relationships, coalitions, coordinating.

We have this stupid thing called loyalty. Work, work, work. Unfortunately, the only way to take care of yourself, not your job, is to gain contacts—out from behind your desk!

Randy and his family moved to a less expensive area of the country where he found a management position in his field.

## Elizabeth

I learned that nothing is promised to you. The job doesn't own you. It's just a means for you to make money…I found I have to take time for my family and not just focus on my job. I am repaying them for helping me when I was down. They stepped up for me. Don't allow people to take advantage of you. I was taken advantage of. I didn't feel appreciated for the job I did.

Since her termination, Elizabeth did some consulting and then found a full-time job.

## Melissa

I learned to work every day like it's your last day. The other thing I learned was never to mistake work for family again. I was on a dream team and really respected and completely trusted my team, even secondary people. I did feel it was a family atmosphere. I will never make that mistake again, because they don't need to stick with you. A company can let you go easily.

Melissa found another position after more than nine months of searching. That position was eliminated and also ended abruptly. She then took on a new career, had additional training, and is now employed full time in her field.

## Nick

> People say losing a job happens to everyone; it happened to me more than once. It's very political, even in churches. People may say you're such a nice guy, but even nice guys get fired. They go to work and get fired. People think it can't happen to him. It can, and it does. I remember telling people when I was still employed, "I will never look for another job or interview for another job." Totally naïve. That's been the learning experience. Leadership is tough. If you are twenty-five and you want to be the leader, there is a cost that comes with it. There are reasons—high risk, high reward. The best way to be prepared is to be ready to bounce.

Nick relocated to gain employment six months following his job loss. At this position Nick realized his department would be let go and proactively sought another job that also required relocation. He works there today.

## Lesley

> I learned that no matter what, you don't want to compromise your character, integrity, or work ethic to conform. I learned that you have to give yourself credit for the part you play in the organization and the value you bring. Don't allow others to bring you down. Give yourself the credit and use it to leverage what you want out of your career.
>
> I learned that sometimes the most genuine of relationships are not with your peers or your boss. It can be with the individuals who are in a front line, or a front-line supervisor. It wasn't at all the people who were on my core team.

The best tidbits of knowledge and advice are in those relationships. I remember a friend in procurement told me everything I did to help her. She was so complimentary. She did so much for my well-being. Things like that keep me going. My boss would call me a Little Mary Sunshine.

Even to this day, five years later, I still have people call me for advice. What should I do? They turn to me. They tell me how they are being treated. They ask if they are being paranoid. I tell them to trust what they see.

Lesley started her own consulting company following her departure. She successfully parlayed that experience into a full-time senior position in her field.

## Joe

You can be doing the best job and be successful, but for reasons beyond your control, you can lose your job. So, I take every opportunity to not take anything for granted.

I also learned that it's very hard to implement change in an organization where there is success. In organizations not doing as well, I could apply my skills and see progress. Innovation occurs in the fringes. It doesn't occur with organizations strong and solid.

Through it all I kept studying, kept learning, kept being involved with organizations that could teach me and get me involved in leadership and management of organizations. Human resources positions were key to all of them. HR was the way to survive in health care and to advance quality, systems, and leadership.

At end of my career, this quality and systems work is coming back in and leadership is less important. How employees are engaged, how people work together—these things are coming to the surface again.

The counselors say, "Look at this as an opportunity. Something is always positive." I can tell you it's not an opportunity. I have learned more. It's never an easy transition. I like to go overboard for success. To be down to a couple candidates and be told you aren't getting the job is so difficult.

Joe was unemployed nearly two years. Since this episode, Joe has been let go two more times, all due to changes in management. Each job change has required relocating his family. He is currently employed full-time in a position similar to his previous ones.

## Mackenzie

I learned that you have to keep your mouth shut. I learned that you should not confide in anyone, vent, or get angry at work. Keep your head down and do your job. People talk, and people can't be trusted. If you want to lose your job, open your mouth.

Mackenzie found a position in the public-school system after leaving her job as a teacher in a private school. She eventually left teaching and returned to civil service.

## Mark

Did I grow? If anything, I developed a level of suspiciousness and distrust that was never in me before. I don't know that that will heal anyone.

Mark works full time in his own consulting business.

## Gail

First, I would say that systems thinking helps to keep things in perspective. That means to keep yourself on the balcony. As a leader you need to look at the system and see what is happening in that system and what your role is. Sometimes you have to disrupt the system and wake others up so they can make the transformation. It's easy to get sucked into the day to day. Leaders have to stay vigilant and not get caught in the status quo. Leaders have to look for the adaptive work by inspiring employees to own it and do it.

It's hard, but I learned to be comfortable with disruption. That often initiates the important transformation that needs to happen.

We create a story for ourselves that our friends need us and can't live without us. Keep your priorities as the main thing. The other things are icing, not the cake.

After completing her degree, Gail made a significant leap to a fast-paced firm and then moved to a senior leadership role in her field.

## Bruce

First, boards and leaders should get a second opinion before deciding to terminate someone. Lawyers want to minimize risk. That is what they will always argue. The board or anyone firing someone should get a second legal opinion.

Second, I learned to beware of human resources and legal. Take a friend of mine—he was fired after more than ten years with his company. His performance evaluation was a month prior to his termination, and it was excellent. Then HR and legal went to the board and told them he was having an affair with a coworker. The board didn't investigate. They took their opinion and fired both. He had to relocate his family to find a new job. And the lawyer ended up becoming the CEO—what a conflict of interest!

Bruce did not find a new position and instead decided to retire.

## Andrew

I learned how to interview, how to speak to others. I learned a
lot. This stuff is not taught anywhere else, and it's not practiced
anywhere else. But you absolutely need to develop these skills to
succeed.

Andrew found a comparable position four months after his job loss. He
credits outplacement services for helping him get ready to interview
for this job.

## Julie

You can't adjust the ocean, but you can adjust your sails.

Julie was out of work for ten months before finding employment. To support her family, she spent all her savings. She had to declare bankruptcy.
She is presently employed full time in her field.

## Kristin

I learned that just because you're young doesn't mean you're
wrong. I don't mean to be arrogant. I mean, in a moral way if
you feel you are being treated wrong, there are hundreds of
jobs. Don't stay in one where you won't be successful, especially
if it's part time or you're in college. I'm not saying to just quit;
there are other jobs. If you are looking, employees have the
best insight into their company. Talk to employees before taking a job.
    I learned quickly how a bad business is run. People should
do their research on who they are working for. You don't have
to take the first job you get. If you have to work, you may have to
withstand some poor treatment. Do your homework.

Kristin found another part-time job and has since graduated from college. This part-time job turned into a full-time position after graduation.

## Mona

I learned a lot. The first thing I learned was who my true friends were. The true friends reached out and offered their support. They weren't afraid to remain friends. They weren't afraid to be seen with me. But there were others who never called or contacted me after I was let go. It hurt. I had worked with them for years, went to their parents' funerals, attended their baby showers, visited them in the hospital, and supported them in their careers. It felt like I was being shunned. Now I know who my true friends are.

Second, I learned to never again emotionally invest in my job and coworkers. I made so many sacrifices because I was loyal. I will be loyal to myself from now on. I will always do a great job, but I won't make my work my family.

Mona worked as a consultant for a few months before joining a company full time.

## Lori

I learned that despite your best efforts, sometimes you can't control the outcome. I learned that even though I haven't always been in my ideal position, my needs have been met. My quality of life has not suffered. That's digging down deep and deciding what's important. My needs were met working two jobs for a few months.

Lori found work in her field but has avoided management positions. She remains gun-shy and afraid of failing.

## Janice

I don't know. It's kind of like…feel comfortable changing jobs. You don't have to stay somewhere forever. Sometimes it's good… I think that all my life I felt I could walk away from any job. It's a comfortable feeling that most people don't have. But I think you need to have something in place so that if things aren't going well, don't make yourself sick staying there. You have to do something else where you will feel good about what you do. Don't stick around if you are unhappy. Whatever job you do, do it well.

Janice worked as a consultant and then found full-time employment with a former colleague.

## Renee

I learned that no one looks out for you but you. My boss's boss didn't intervene. I thought she would. But she didn't help me. She just let her new person do what she wanted. I learned no one helps you but you. It doesn't matter that you had great evaluations, that you were there twenty-seven years, that you won an international award. None of that matters. It doesn't matter. What matters is letting the boss do what she wants. I learned my lesson. Now I know. Now I know you have to look out for yourself.

Renee found work in another department within her company.

## Don

I learned to always obey the Lord. Seek His will and know it well before making a move forward, backward, to the left, or right. Pray and listen for the Lord's will. Do not try to take action on your own, and look to the Lord to bless your choice.

Don found work after six months, which required relocating his family. He has since found another position in the same area.

## Wes

> After the fellow I worked for and another guy were pushed out, I think I should have been more proactive and started the process of leaving on my own. I kind of felt the sense of loyalty, a false sense of loyalty, that leaving them was somehow wrong. It is definitely an attitude I don't want to repeat. It was probably my fault. If the boss wants you to be one way, you should be that way or look for an alternative position.
>
> There were two bosses; I fell into the camp that was out of favor. If I really wanted to stay, I should have been more aggressive about earning the good graces of my boss. I should have kissed up to him more. But I am not that kind of person. Looking back, I should have started the search on my own.

After more than a year searching, Wes took a job with a small company through a friend of a friend.

## Alexa

> In the future, I need to get to know the company culture and see if I fit there. Now I know moving forward, my research will be not only about clients and quality of the work they produce, but about how they treat one another, are they friends, and do they treat people like human beings?
>
> I want a smaller agency where the company culture is more important, where they want people to do well and enjoy what they do. Not just eating people up, like in a big company.
>
> If you feel like it's not right, there is no need to stick with it just because you feel like you can't leave. Looking back, I felt I couldn't quit, but I wish I had. I wish I had beaten them to the

punch. Don't stay where you are so unhappy. I felt I had to stay. I felt I had to finish.

Alexa is living at home with her parents while she searches for her next job.

## Diane

Do not trust anyone. Do not stay anywhere for twenty-eight years. Work somewhere where there is protection. Do what is best for you.

A friend of Diane's told her about a position in a similar company. Diane stayed in that position and went back to school to get a teaching certificate. She now teaches full time.

## Kate

Never let anyone carry your ball.

Kate started her own company, where she continues five years later as its CEO.

## Key Takeaways

1. No one looks out for you but you. Do what is best for you.
2. Don't stay in a job if you can't be successful.
3. Be true to yourself and don't compromise your character.
4. It can happen to you.

# CHAPTER 14

## REFLECTIONS

With hundreds of hours interviewing, hundreds more coding, and untold hours writing and editing, I became completely immersed in the data from my interviews. I stepped away from the book for a few months and gave myself time to reflect and think. I needed to get my head out of the weeds. Then I asked myself the same question I asked my participants: "What did you learn?" It took some time to distill my thoughts. Here are my reflections, which I have organized from both the employee and organizational perspective.

## What Have I Learned from the Employee's Perspective?

We work for many reasons, including the need to support ourselves and our families. For most of us, our health care, and that of our family, is often tied to our work. There is a lot at stake. So first and foremost, I think we need to change our mind-sets. No longer can we expect to keep a job and advance through a single organization. We cannot hold stock with the notion of a future with a given company, even when we are doing a fantastic job and receiving recognition for it. Too many things can change. Many of my interviewees learned this lesson the hard way.

The company you work in may not have a future either. For one, our environment is fluid. Automation has ended many jobs, outsourcing has ended others. Mergers and acquisitions have also led to job loss through consolidation. Globalization has had a significant impact on jobs in the United States. Innovation itself can lead to significant changes in our work lives. The impact of artificial intelligence has not been realized. Who knows what is next?

And as if this uncertainty isn't enough, e*mployment at will* is standard operating procedure (and the law) in many states. An employer needs no reason to let someone go. As employees, we all need to remember that. The people I met considered themselves loyal to their organizations and the people in them. Most of them never imagined they were vulnerable and had no intentions of leaving their employers. As such, they didn't pursue other opportunities. They admittedly didn't network as much as they should have. They didn't save for a rainy day. So how do we remain solid, enthusiastic performers in our organizations and at the same time prepare for a possible job loss? We have to have our feet in both worlds.

It may be time to be loyal to ourselves as much as our employers. Instead of looking at all we are *doing for* the employer, we could choose to look at the skills, education and training, connections, benefits and pay we are *gaining* from our employers. We should probably view each job as a training ground for the next opportunity, rather than a permanent home. With this attitude, we look at what the employer and the job can do for us in addition to thinking what we are doing for them. That doesn't mean it won't be a shock and a disappointment to lose that job, or that it won't be difficult to get a new one, it just means our mind-set is different. Your job can provide the opportunity to build your portfolio and your connections. *Take advantage of these opportunities while you have them.*

That leads to a second thought: we need to remember it is not disloyal to check out other job opportunities or respond to headhunters. As many of the people in this book said, our first loyalty needs to be to ourselves and our families. Checking out another position allows you to get a pulse on the job market and your attractiveness in it. A friend of mine says, "You have to have three on the line," meaning three potential job opportunities. And as the saying goes, "Never let the ink dry on your résumé."

Third, usually there are signs that a job loss is forthcoming. The people I interviewed invariably could describe these signs in great detail, although usually in hindsight. Pay attention to what is going on at work.

Are people avoiding you? Are your responsibilities reduced? Are you on the wrong side of office politics? Are you outperforming your peers or your boss? Did you get a new leader? These signs and others described by the participants may not be guarantee a job loss is coming, but they should at least signal caution.

Fourth, we cannot underestimate the potential impact of a getting a new leader. This was the most pronounced and striking finding of my research. In this study, the most frequent precursor to losing a job was getting a new supervisor. Indeed, slightly more than half of the terminations I studied occurred shortly after the employee got a new supervisor. And it seemed to be a big surprise when it happened. The employees had been told for years that they were doing a good job. Many were promoted or given an award. They felt comfortable and knew what was expected of them. In their minds, they had learned how to do what the boss wanted. When a new leader arrived, none of that counted anymore.

Often in these situations, the new boss had different expectations, different ways of doing things, and different communication patterns than the previous one. Subsequently, there is a *disconnect* for the employee, who has been doing his or her job the same way for usually more than a year. This is especially true for those who had the support of their prior supervisors. People can be caught between what has made them successful and what a new leader views as necessary to be successful. However, the employees interviewed maintained that they were continuing to do things the right way for the company. With a new leader, what had made them successful and recognized no longer worked.

In other cases, it is the organization's norm to allow the new person to bring in his or her own team. Organizations tend to give their new managers a lot of rope to get the job done, including replacing incumbents. Leaders know that other leaders get things done with people they know and trust.

As employees, we need to keep our radars finely tuned. Transitions are tough. We need to be prepared for the consequences of a new leader. Most importantly, we need to take it upon ourselves to build a relationship with a new leader and listen carefully to his or her goals and directions. Although it is tempting, saying, "We don't do it that way" is not a recipe for success.

Fifth, our eyes need to be wide open before taking a new job. A new job is challenging because it involves understanding a new leader, a new culture, and a new system. All three at once. As the Leadership IQ study points out, 50 percent of new hires don't work out in the first eighteen months. Recall that survey showed the biggest reason for termination was that the new employee was *not a fit* for the organization's culture. New employees are likely eager to jump in and make a good impression. But that may not be wise. If the biggest reason for being let go from a new job is that you are not a "culture fit," it would seem that the most important thing you can do when joining a new organization is to intentionally observe and understand the culture. That means finding out how things get done, assessing the power structure, and watching for informal rules before you step in it or inadvertently offend someone. It will require that you be more guarded and less engaged. You probably already know what you are doing and have the skills needed for the new position. What you don't have yet is an understanding of the culture. Relationship building is the key task in starting a new job. For the first three months, try to focus on understanding the leader and the company's culture. And I bet many of you thought all you had to do was do a good job.

Sixth, it seems that we all need to be more flexible, nimbler, more able to adapt to changing circumstances. Trends are not invisible. We all know about globalization, automation, and consolidation. It's even got an acronym, VUCA—volatility, uncertainty, complexity, and ambiguity. Our new normal *should* be job uncertainty—there is no longer job security. We usually don't know when or how, but we do know that many factors can render one jobless. Like the companies we work for, we need to be able to turn on a dime.

So we need to be proactive. We need to have a plan B *and* a plan C. And the best time to develop a backup plan is when you are employed. A backup plan may take many forms. You have heard all your life to save for a rainy day. In this era of job uncertainty, this is essential. Be sure you have saved enough to weather a period—at least six months—without a salary. In addition, take steps now to pay off your house and other debts, thereby reducing your monthly expenses. Unemployment, while helpful, does not make up for a lost salary.

Another plan B might be to look at starting a part-time or home-based business. Whether it's working as a part-time high school coach or becoming a sales consultant for a cosmetic company, having that other source of income may come in handy one day. Also, if your spouse or partner is not in the workforce with paid employment, consider asking them to. A family with two incomes has greater protection from job loss and the costly expense of health insurance. Or, maybe it's time to go back to school to learn new skills or achieve a more marketable degree. The people in this study employed all these strategies and recommend that you hedge your bets or have a plan B.

We can play offense as well.

It is important to maintain healthy relationships and continue networking. It is a fact that most jobs are found through networking. That should not start when you are unemployed. It needs to be a proactive activity. Networking conjures up the image of people using other people to get ahead. That's not what I mean. For networking to be effective, it needs to be sincere. There has to be give and take, trust and relationship building. That means building social capital throughout your life.

Finally, a shift in thinking is in order. Instead of believing that we will always have a full-time job, we may need to anticipate that there will be breaks in our employment. We may have periods of unemployment, part-time work, or contract work. This is a new mind-set. By thinking this way, we are forced to do some contingency planning. That thinking may lead you to a second or third career. A hobby may turn into a job or a new business.

*Job uncertainty is the new normal.* We have to take responsibility for ourselves and our families. We cannot be complacent. We need to be prepared.

## What Have I Learned from an Organizational Perspective?

I have given a lot of thought to the disconnect between the need for skilled employees, the amount of turnover, and open positions in the workforce. Reading the Leadership IQ study, I found it alarming that only 11 percent of people are let go due to the lack of skills for the job.

*That means in most cases, employees were terminated who had the skills to do the job.* The other 89 percent of people were let go due to personality characteristics. If lack of coachability is a reason for termination, maybe it isn't just the employee who can't learn; maybe it's the supervisor who doesn't have time or doesn't know how to coach. If motivation is a problem, again, maybe the organization could share some of the responsibility for helping supervisors motivate and encourage their new employees more. I'm not naïve, but I ask myself, how do we know that the next group of employees will do better than the ones we just let go? And ultimately, is it OK to take away someone's livelihood because of his or her personality? Maybe sometimes it is, other times maybe not.

I also wonder if organizations could not be more thoughtful and conscientious about bringing in new people. One way is to be more diligent in the hiring process. That means looking closely for a cultural fit as well as a technical fit. Having a newly hired person lose his or her job because the company made a hiring mistake is an unnecessary hardship for both parties.

In addition, there must be a better way of helping new employees transition successfully to their new companies. The problem of fit should not be solely the new person's job. Helping new employees avoid political gaffs and sacred cows is one way to help. Starting a new job can be overwhelming. Onboarding that goes beyond parking and lunch breaks, policies and procedures, and the actual job duties is desperately needed if employers want to retain effective employees.

In this research, getting a new boss was found to be a very high predictor of being let go. It's understandable that a company wants to empower its new leader to get results. By leader, I actually mean supervisor, or anyone with direct reports. And it makes sense that a company wants to learn from a new leader's experiences. I am curious, though, if there isn't more an organization can do to prepare its team members for a new supervisor and likewise, prepare its new supervisors for their incumbent team members. This might be one of the most important things employers can do to build employee trust and engagement.

As said earlier, the majority of the people in this study experienced a change in supervisor shortly before being let go. They also expressed that prior to this new leader, they were a valued employee with strong performance reviews and accolades. Why does someone work well with one leader and not another? What happened to change the company's perception of this employee? And, are we confident that our new leaders have the capacity to evaluate their new employees fairly? It might be good for the organization to look closely into a new manager's suggested changes before approving terminations. Perhaps the new leader might be encouraged to take ninety days of so to assess his or her team before making changes.

It also occurs to me that some employees had previous supervisors who themselves lacked leadership and coaching skills. So their employees may have been given a false impression of what is involved with the job and what doing a good job means. A new supervisor comes in with different standards and expectations. The employees learn they are not doing a good job, and to do a good job, it needs to be done in this new way. Those who can't adapt are likely to be let go.

Another question to consider from this research is how can we handle terminations more humanely? For example, is the perp walk necessary? Is it essential that an employee immediately give up his or her badge, computer, and keys? I recognize sometimes these measures are essential—the employer has to protect itself and its remaining employees. And with some offenses, it's nonnegotiable. But, isn't it better for both the employer and the employee to have a more civil process? One of my acquaintances likes to say, "Red carpet in, red carpet out." A dignified, gracious exit would likely have better outcomes for both parties.

And even though employment at will is the law in most states, wouldn't it be better to provide the employee some warning or feedback that he or she is not living up to expectations? So many of the people I interviewed said they had no warning and no due process. Just because there is employment at will doesn't mean that it should be invoked unchecked.

Last, I encourage anyone who is a manager or human resource professional to take great care in using his or her power. The stories in this book are compelling and in many cases heartbreaking. The loss of employment impacts more than just the employee. Work is integral to financial, physical, and emotional well-being of a family. Knowing the impact of unemployment, are there ways we as leaders can be more responsive and sensitive to those who are applying for positions in our organizations? People I interviewed told me about the dozens of positions they applied for and how frustrating the lack of response was. They said they just wanted an answer—is the company interested in them or not. Can we find better ways of humanizing what can be a very dehumanizing process?

The power that managers and human resource professionals hold is also heightened at the time of employee termination. In situations where there is no drastic misdeed or violation, would it be feasible for organizations to help the employee with an exit strategy and story? Is there a better way to help those being let go have a softer landing, retain their dignity, and be poised to move on? Likewise, is there a better way to communicate someone's departure than the abrupt e-mail saying the individual is no longer employed? In my research, I have heard from tenured employees who were let go during the day and perp-walked out the door without a chance to even go back to their desks. I also heard stories of employees who were offered the opportunity to craft and exit story along with their employers and communicate it upon their departure. Some even were given prior notice of their termination so that they could begin looking for new work. Their colleagues got to say goodbye and wish them well. Are there risks with this? Of course. Would this approach work for every employee to be let go? Of course not.

When possible, I believe a better, kinder way of handling departures is needed. A dignified approach demonstrates the company's sensitivity and goodwill to its stakeholders. As we heard from our interviewees, terminations and layoffs promote fear, anger, and rumors in the workplace and even in the community. Harsh treatment does not help either party. If an employee is treated with civility, empathy, and respect, perhaps the harm done to the organization and the individual would be minimized.

And then again, maybe not. But if employee engagement and retention is the organization's goal, these suggestions might be worth a try.

# APPENDIX
## METHODOLOGY

## Introduction

This book is an example of qualitative research. The strengths of qualitative research include a focus of words over numbers and a focus on people, stories, and situations. The key to qualitative research is its focus on the lives, actions, and experiences of people. Using this method, the researcher can better understand how participants think and feel about the situation and what it means to them. In addition, qualitative research provides context and process to the events the participants describe. Qualitative research stands on its own merit but is also used to determine what questions to study in quantitative research.

Quantitative research then focuses on numbers—frequencies, averages, correlations, and so on. It is considered objective. Quantitative research collects and analyzes numerical data from a study attempts to explain or understand a phenomenon.

In my research for this book, I spoke to more than sixty-five individuals who have been fired, laid off, or had their jobs eliminated. I spoke to several others who shared the story of someone they knew who was let go. During the initial phase of data collection, I conducted informal, unstructured conversations with people who had involuntarily lost their jobs. For this preliminary research I had no interview guide; I just listened to their stories and documented our conversations. This phase involved twenty-five people.

These conversations became the foundation of my research. Based on them I developed an interview guide. I then conducted in-depth interviews with forty people. Although I developed an order of questions, the participants' responses did not neatly follow the interview guide. In fact, they usually just told me their stories.

## Consent and Anonymity

Each of the participants gave their consent to be interviewed. I assured them of confidentiality and anonymity. All the interviewees were told that their participation was voluntary and that they could stop at any time. No one stopped the conversation; in fact, most people found it helpful to talk with someone about it.

Due to the extremely sensitive and personal nature of the subject, as well as my desire to protect both the individuals interviewed and the companies involved, I concealed their identities. I have disguised even those who gave me full permission to use their real names (many did) and disclose their companies' identities. I declined the offer, saying I would only use their stories under the condition of anonymity. Anonymity is important for both the individual and the company.

Sadly, though fortunate for my research, finding people to interview was easy. Through personal and professional contacts and networking also known as convenience sampling, I found the first set of respondents. This group provided the basis for the initial informal conversations and unstructured interviews. Then I used snowball sampling: I asked people I interviewed to refer me to others they knew who might be willing to be interviewed. "You should talk to so-and-so" was a common response I got after interviewing someone or after telling him or her the nature of my research. No one declined to be interviewed. In addition, I would tell people what my book was about as I was investigating publishing options. Almost invariably, they would convey to me that the topic was important and that either they personally or someone they knew had just gone through a job loss. This too provided additional subjects.

The research took place over a period of five years. It was difficult to stop the data collection phase of this project as I continued to identify new participants with powerful stories.

I spoke to my participants by phone or in person. Two individuals chose to answer the questions in writing. Three others supplemented their interviews with additional written information. The interviewees came from twelve different states representing all regions of the United States. Their former companies were diverse as well: insurance, financial services, energy, sports and entertainment, health care, safety, manufacturing, human services, law, and technology. Subjects ranged from twenty to sixty-two years of age. All but two were exempt employees.

To be sure I accurately captured each person's words, intentions, and meaning, I listened carefully and created verbatim transcripts of the interviews. To clarify meaning, I repeated back to them what I heard them say. This served to confirm or to correct what was said. Moreover, in doing so the respondents often added more to their responses. People think and react at different speeds, so it was important to allow them the time to fully explore and develop their responses.

I was able to record each person's story of losing his or her job, coping with that loss, and what he or she learned from the experience. Stories provide an excellent way to take the reader into the lives of the research participants. Stories also convey overall meanings and concepts related to the experience being studied. And, in their book, *Composing Qualitative Research,* Biddle and Locke state, "The distinguishing characteristic of stories is that they possess a discernible framework for structuring the written account. Specifically, stories are grounded in events and provide a narrative structure that organizes those events into beginnings, middles and ends." This book's organization follows that structure with three sections: the event of being fired, coping with job loss, and finally reflections and advice.

## Triangulation

To build a context for these stories, I also spoke to their spouses, children, and former coworkers. Human resource professionals, headhunters, and outplacement counselors also shared their perspectives. In addition, I have incorporated examples of terminations reported in the media. Many public and even a few private figures have had their terminations covered in the media. I pepper this book with their stories to further illustrate a pattern or point. In research this is called triangulation. Triangulation serves to check bias by offering multiple sources of data. Many of these examples may be familiar to the reader, but hopefully they will shed additional light on the subject.

## Coding and Thematic Analysis

The book organizes the interviewees' responses into common themes. In his book *Transforming Qualitative Information*, Richard Boyatzis defines thematic analysis "as a way of seeing things. Often what one sees through thematic analysis does not appear to others, even if they are observing the same information, events, or situations." Further Dr. Boyatzis describes the process of conducting a thematic analysis, "Recognizing an important moment (seeing), precedes encoding (seeing it as something) which in turn precedes interpretation. Thematic analysis moves you through these three phases of inquiry."

After data gathering, I read and reread each interview transcript several times. I used open coding to identify commonalities and themes in the participants' stories. I repeated this process so as to capture themes as comprehensively as possible. I then arranged my notes to put together passages of interviews with similar themes. I also organized my notes by the questions on my interview guide. In most cases participants did not answer questions in an orderly way, one at a time, but rather wove their stories as they wanted to. I then looked for answers to each question and compiled them together. I did not use a coding software program; rather I coded all the interviews manually. Doing so helped me more deeply absorb and understand their meanings.

For example, all the participants responded to my question about how they were notified they would lose their jobs. I have combined their clearly identified responses into one chapter of this book so the reader can get a broad picture of how the terminations occurred. Similarly, another chapter shares the respondents' job-seeking advice, and so on. I provide some analysis and weave together their experiences.

This book includes inductive methods of qualitative research, meaning that I began without a theoretical base. This means that I was not trying to look at this data through a theoretical lens. I wanted to write something that would be professionally accepted yet accessible to the public.

It is understood with qualitative research that memories are subject to incomplete and inaccurate recollections. The interviewees often re-called new details and stories of their separation when answering other questions. And speaking about their job losses also provoked some mem-ories they previously had not identified.

## Personal Interest

I have a personal interest in this topic. I watched each of my parents lose their jobs and struggle emotionally and practically. It was frightening and traumatic for our family. I personally have been on both sides of the firing line. What began with personal experiences led me to informal conversations. These stories moved me and motivated me to learn more. That led to this qualitative research study using methods of formal, semi-structured interviews. The research was truly organic in nature.

# Recommended Reading

Brzezinski, Mika. 2010. *Knowing Your Value*. New York: Weinstein Books.

Hoffman, Reid, Ben Casnocha, and Chris Yeh. 2014. *The Alliance: Managing Talent in the Networked Age*. Boston: Harvard Business Review Press.

Pearce, Jone. 2006, 2007. *Organizational Behavior: Real Research for Real Managers*. Irvine: Melvin and Leigh.

Pugh, Allison. 2016. *The Tumbleweed Society: Working and Caring in an Age of Insecurity*. New York: Oxford University Press.
Schenck, Dwain. 2014. *Reset*. Boston: Da Capo Press.

Willyerd, Karie, and Barbara Mistick. 2016. *Stretch: How to Future-Proof Yourself for Tomorrow's Workplace*. Hoboken: Wiley Publishing.

# References

## Introduction

Bureau of Labor Statistics. "Job Openings, Hires and Separations Return to Prerecession Levels in 2015." JOLTS. Accessed September 2016. https://www.bls.gov/opub/mlr/2016/article/job-openings-hires-and-separations-return-to-prerecession-levels-in-2015.htm.

Future Workplace. "Multiple Generations @Work" survey. http://futureworkplace.com/wp-content/uploads/MultipleGenAtWork_infographic.pdf.

Gallup Daily poll. March 5, 2017. http://www.gallup.com/home.aspx.

Hoffman, Reid, Ben Casnocha, and Chris Yeh. 2014. *The Alliance: Managing Talent in the Networked Age.* Boston: Harvard Business Review Press.

Murphy, Mark. 2012. "Hiring for Attitude: Research and Tools to Skyrocket Your Success Rate." Leadership IQ.

O'Donnell, J. T. 2015. "3 Reasons Millennials Are Getting Fired." *Inc.*

Pearce, Jone. 2006, 2007. *Organizational Behavior: Real Research for Real Managers.* Irvine: Melvin and Leigh.

Pugh, Allison. 2016. *The Tumbleweed Society: Working and Caring in an Age of Insecurity.* New York: Oxford University Press.

Terkel, Studs. 1974. *Working: People Talk About What They Do All Day and How They Feel About What They Do.* New York: The New Press.

## Chapter 1
*The Apprentice* (2004) and *The Celebrity Apprentice* (2017). NBC. www.nbc.com.

Biden, Joe. September 1, 2016. Speech given in Warren, Ohio. https://www.c-span.org/video/?414632-1/joe-biden-campaigns-hillary-clinton-warren-ohio.

*CBS This Morning.* August 12, 2013. "AOL CEO Fires Employee on Conference Call." https://www.youtube.com/watch?v=2ZaEgbQhrMc.

Glass, Andrew. 2008. "Reagan Fires 11,000 Striking Air Traffic Controllers." August 5, 1981. *Politico.*

Pearce, Jone. 2006, 2007. *Organizational Behavior: Real Research for Real Managers.* Irvine: Melvin and Leigh.

Shear, Michael D., and Matt Apuzzo. 2017. "FBI Director James Comey Is Fired by Trump." *New York Times.*

Whitaker, Bill. 2017. "You're Fired." *60 Minutes.* CBS.

## Chapter 2
Malloy, Tim. 2014. "Fox News' Chris Wallace Derides NBC's Lousy Treatment of David Gregory." The Wrap.

Michael, Paul. 2007. "You're Fired! 20 Signs That a Pink Slip is Coming." Wise Bread Picks. Updated April 15, 2011.

Murphy, Mark. 2015. "Why New Hires Fail (Emotional Intelligence vs. Skills)." Leadership IQ blog. http://www.leadershipiq.com/blogs/leadershipiq/35354241-why-new-hires-fail-emotional-intelligence-vs-skills.

Patrick, Patricia A. 2010. "Be Prepared Before You Blow the Whistle." *Fraud* magazine.

## Chapter 3
Rudin, Ken. 2007. "The Eagleton Fiasco of 1972." National Public Radio. http://www.npr.org/templates/story/story.php?storyId=7755888.

Schroeder, George. 2013. "College Football Proved to Be Gordon Gee's Undoing." *USA Today.*

Stanley, Alessandra. 2012. "Farewell, Without a Parachute; Ann Curry's Tearful Goodbye from 'Today.'" *New York Times.*

Thomas, Evan. 2005. "The Government Response to Katrina: A Disaster within a Disaster." *Newsweek.* http://www.newsweek.com/government-response-katrina-disaster-within-disaster-118257.

## Chapter 4
*Wall Street.* 1987. Film. Directed by Oliver Stone. Produced by Twentieth Century Fox and American Entertainment Partners LP, produced in association with Amercent Films.

## Chapter 5
*Burn Notice.* 2007–2013. USA network. http://www.usanetwork.com/burnnotice.

# Chapter 6

Beavers, Olivia. 2017. "FBI Employees Wear 'Comey Is My Homey' T-Shirts to Family Day." MSN. https://www.msn.com/en-us/news/politics/fbi-employees-wear-%E2%80%98comey-is-my-homey%E2%80%99-t-shirts-to-family-day/ar-BBDH3XQ?li=BBnbcA1.

Campbell, James. 2017. "James Comey Is No Showboat." *USA Today.* https://www.usatoday.com/story/opinion/2017/06/08/james-comey-bigger-than-russia-donald-trump-testimony-column/102562824/.

Erdley, Debra, and Bill Zlatos. 2013. "Upheaval at Heinz Endowments Raises Eyebrows:

Son Exerted Control When Teresa Heinz Kerry Was Ill." *Pittsburgh Tribune-Review.*

Pearce, Jone. 2006, 2007. *Organizational Behavior: Real Research for Real Managers.* Irvine: Melvin and Leigh.

Ibid., 141–2.

Rozsa, Matthew. 2017. "FBI Employee: James Comey's Firing Has Caused 'Anger' among Agents." Salon.com. http://www.salon.com/2017/06/08/fbi-special-agent-james-comeys-firing-has-caused-anger-among-agents/.

Stetler, Brian. 2016. "Who Can Save the 'Today' Show?" *New York Times.* http://www.nytimes.com/2013/04/21/magazine/whocansavethetodayshow.

*Today* show. Television. 2012. NBC. June 28, 2012

Zlatos, Bill, and Debra Erdley. 2013. "Heinz Staff Shift Linked to Chief's Son." TribLive.

## Chapter 7

Calfas, Jennifer. 2017. "Getting Fired Can Feel Worse Than Losing a Spouse." *Money*.

Hamlish, Marvin, and Edward Kleban. 1975. "What I Did for Love." *A Chorus Line*.

Miller, Arthur. 1949. *Death of a Salesman*. Penguin Plays.

Morin, Rich, and Rakesh Kochhar. 2010. "Lost Income, Lost Friends and Loss of Self-Respect." Pew Research Center. http://www.pewsocial-trends.org/2010/07/22/hard-times-have-hit-nearly-everyone-and-hammered-the-long-term-unemployed/.

Pew Research Center. 2008. "You're Laid Off: A Worsening Economy Couldn't Come at a Worse Time for Many US Workers." http://www.pewsocialtrends.org/2008/04/16/youre-laid-off/.

Pugh, Allison. 2016. *The Tumbleweed Society: Working and Caring in an Age of Insecurity*. New York: Oxford University Press.


## Chapter 8

O'Brien, Conan. 2016. "Conan O'Brien Remembers Garry Shandling." *Conan*. TBS. https://www.youtube.com/watch?v=DMsVfEqLFiI.


## Chapter 9

Claman, Patricia. 2012. "HBR Guide to Getting the Right Job." *Harvard Business Review*.

Knight, Rebecca. 2015. "How to Bounce Back After Getting Laid Off." *Harvard Business Review*. https://hbr.org/2015/07/how-to-bounce-back-after-getting-laid-off.

Lees, John. 2014. *How to Get a Job You Love.* New York: McGraw Hill, 8th edition.

## Chapter10

The Friday Hangout. 2014. www.fridayhangout.com featuring Jill Rowley on social selling. Post has been removed.

Hoffman, Reid, Ben Casnocha, and Chris Yeh. 2014a. "Your Company Is Not a Family." *Harvard Business Review.*

Hoffman, Reid, Ben Casnocha, and Chris Yeh. 2014b. "The Alliance: Managing Talent in the Networked Age." *Harvard Business Review.*

Pugh, Allison. 2016. *The Tumbleweed Society: Working and Caring in an Age of Insecurity.* New York: Oxford University Press.

Soskey, Ginny. 2014. "Sales Queen Jill Rowley Shares the 5 Pillars of #SocialSelling." HubSpot. http://blog.hubspot.com/sales/social-selling-jill-rowley.

## Chapter 11

Acuff, Jon. 2015. *Do Over: Rescue Monday, Reinvent Your Work, and Never Get Stuck.* Portfolio.

Cornell University's Career Center. "Networking." http://www.career.cornell.edu/students/options/networking/.

Doyle, Alison. 2017. "Résumé Keywords and Tips for Using Them." The Balance. https://www.thebalance.com/resume-keywords-and-tips-for-using-them-2063331.

Granovetter, Mark. 1973. "The Strength of Weak Ties." *American Journal of Sociology,* (1360–80).

TheLadders. *Keeping an Eye on Recruiter Behavior.* http://cdn.theladders.net/static/images/basicSite/pdfs/TheLadders-EyeTracking-StudyC2.pdf.

Morgan, Hannah. 2014. "Don't Believe These 8 Job Search Myths." *US News.* http://money.usnews.com/money/blogs/outsidevoicescareers/2014/09/17/dontbelievethese8jobsearchmyths.

Sullivan, John. 2013. "Why You Can't Get A Job…Recruiting Explained By the Numbers." Talent Function Group LLC. www.ere.net.

Sullivan, Kate. 2015. "How to Bounce Back After Being Fired." *Women's Health.* http://www.womenshealthmag.com/life/what-to-do-if-youre-fired.

United States Department of Labor. 2017. "Job Openings and Labor Turnover Summary." https://www.bls.gov/news.release/jolts.nr0.htm.

Willyerd, Karie, and Barbara Mistick. 2016. *Stretch: How to Future-Proof Yourself for Tomorrow's Workplace.* Hoboken: Wiley Publishing.

## Appendix 1: Methodology

Boyatzis, Richard E. 1998. *Transforming Qualitative Information.* Thousand Oaks: Sage Publications, p. 1.

Golden-Biddle, Karen, and Karen Locke. 1997. *Composing Qualitative Research.* Thousand Oaks: Sage Publications, p. xvi.

Maxwell, Joseph A. 1996. *Qualitative Research Design.* Thousand Oaks: Sage Publications.